VOICES *of*
VETCH FIELD

VOICES *of*
VETCH FIELD

KEITH HAYNES & PHIL SUMBLER

This book is dedicated to the memory of Terry Cole who died tragically on Saturday 6 May 2000
going to watch his team play – a Swansea fan who went to a game and never came home.
Rest in peace Terry, we will never forget you.

The History Press

Keith Haynes is managed and represented by Sheila Willicombe, Elite Management, 43-47 Eaton Road, Brynhyfryd, Swansea SA5 95X; tel 01792 463766/0117 9147604; e-mail sheila@welshstars.co.uk.

First published in 2000 by Tempus Publishing Limited
Reprinted 2004

Reprinted in 2011 by
The History Press
The Mill, Brimscombe Port,
Stroud, Gloucestershire, GL5 2QG
www.thehistorypress.co.uk

British Library Cataloguing in Publication Data.
A catalogue record for this book is available from the British Library.

ISBN 978 0 7524 1592 5

Typesetting and origination by Tempus Publishing Limited.
Printed and bound in Great Britain by
Marston Book Services Limited, Didcot

Contents

Introduction

I was warned at a young age that a life spent supporting the Swans would not be a very rewarding one; that was in 1976. Indeed, it was not a particularly rewarding experience at the time, but little did we know then that Harry Griffiths had assembled a Swans side that would later yield such greats as Jeremy Charles, Alan Curtis and of course Robbie James. The touch paper had been lit by Harry and the rest, as you will read here, is history.

However, the Swans' story is more than those few years of glory when John Toshack led us to the old First Division for the 1981/82 season. We have assembled here some interesting quotes and memories from the people that really matter, the fans. This book includes anecdotes from people of all backgrounds and all ages that support Swansea City.

There are no football politics here, just fond memories, accompanied by pictures of the time that will no doubt send you on your way with that warm feeling we all get as supporters of Swansea – be it Town or City. There are no apologies either, we just couldn't fit in every occasion and every memory – that is a testament to how great this club has been. One book could not cover all the great Swansea moments. We have tried a few new angles and a few different approaches to the usual format of histories, and we hope you like it. If there is a story missing, well, can you write it down?

My own memories, like many others, are of a Swans team at the very top of the old First Division and the headlines on the Saturday night national news as we conquered another supposedly great team from England at The Vetch Field. A particular highlight was that famous drubbing of Leeds United, with five seriously decent goals all fired in to the Leeds net in front of 24,000 dazed and happy Swansea fans at the start of that memorable season. The defeats of Manchester United and Arsenal, Manchester City despatched with such clinical awareness it was frightening, and of course those fondest of memories, beating the Bluebirds of Cardiff on so many occasions it became embarrassing. Remember the snow and the orange ball? It was 4-1 that night to the team in white – Cardiff City were obliterated, and it could have been so many more … but 4-1 will do for now.

Then there was the Autoglass Trophy final defeat of Huddersfield in 1994 and our first Wembley appearance; how fitting that 50,000 people shared that memory – it seemed that the whole of football history had been re-written, and for us it had.

The dark days are here too – 1985 and the death of Swansea City: our club £106,000 in debt and John Bond, Swansea manager, sacked. The players were no longer ours, they belonged to the Football League. A last minute bid in the high court by Douglas Sharpe, later to be chairman and owner, saved us as our fixtures were reinstated at the very last minute. How happy a Christmas that was! I admit that I cried when I heard the Swans had gone, I cried again when they came back. I can only compare it to being told that a very dear friend had died and then to be told it was all a mistake. That's how much it means, that's how much it still means – to all of us.

At the beginning of the twenty-first century we expect greater things for our club, and they are on the horizon, but we still watch our team from the decaying terraces of the North Bank instead of the pristine seats of a new stadium like so many clubs have these days. Maybe that fine championship winning team of the new century can give us hope? However, those terraces and seats of old Vetch Field have so many stories to tell. No journalist could write these psalms of joy that are Swansea City, no writer could forget these words – they are from the heart, they are from us, they are from the fans.

These are our memories, and they are here forever.

The Voices from Vetch Field are alive.

Keith Haynes
October 2000

You'll never walk alone ... when you're with the travelling Swans.

Foreword by Wyndham Evans

Considering the amount of people involved at The Vetch Field these past years, I feel honoured to be asked by Keith Haynes to write the foreword to this excellent new book on Swansea City. The title says it all. At the time of writing Swansea City are champions of Division Three, and Division Two beckons us onwards. Congratulations go to John Hollins, Alan Curtis and all the players and staff. It is an outstanding achievement.

Anyone who has played for the Swans at the Vetch will tell you of the special feeling that engrosses you when you play there. I spent my entire football playing career at Swansea, that's seventeen years, and I enjoyed every minute of it. Of course, supporting the Swans is never dull – it's like a rollercoaster ride – but I can honestly say you will never find a more passionate football fan than a Swansea City supporter. The two Wembley trips in recent years, for two brilliant finals, were two of the most enjoyable days out I have had watching football. The passion and noise generated by the fans was unforgettable.

The football history that has been made at the Vetch these past years is unforgettable too. The lives and memories of thousands of people past and present, players like Charles, Allchurch, James, Medwin, Paul, Griffiths, Herbie Williams, Brian Evans, Tosh, Curt, Robbie, Speedy, Jimmy, Ante, Leighton, Walker, Freestone, Melville, Bound, Smith, Cusack, Roberts, Coates and Hollins.

To Keith and Phil, good luck with this book. To the Vetch it should soon be 'goodbye' as progress, as it must do, takes us to a new stadium. To everyone involved with the Swans enjoy this book, I know it will be a success, and remember 'You will never beat the Swans'.

We will always be – Swansea till we die.

Wyndham Evans, a true Swan

The Squads

Swansea City

Liverpool 1974 Cup Winners

Swansea City	Liverpool 1974 Cup Winners
DAVID STEWART	RAY CLEMENCE
WYNDHAM EVANS	TOMMY SMITH
DZEMAL HADZIABDIC	EMLYN HUGHES
BRIAN ATTLEY	LARRY LLOYD
DAVE RUSHBURY	PHIL THOMPSON
NIGEL STEVENSON	JOEY JONES
LEIGHTON PHILLIPS	ALEC LINDSAY
DUDLEY LEWIS	BRIAN HALL
JOHN MAHONEY	PETER CORMACK
NEIL ROBINSON	PHIL BOERSMA
TOMMY CRAIG	KEVIN KEEGAN
JEREMY CHARLES	JOHN TOSHACK
ANTE RAJKOVIC	STEVE HEIGHWAY
ALAN CURTIS	
DAVID GILES	
ROBBIE JAMES	
LEIGHTON JAMES	

Referee: **HOWARD KING** (Merthyr)

Linesmen: **LEN PEWSEY**(Llanelli, Orange Flag); **VINCE HOWELLS**(Llanelli, Red Flag).

Graham Harcourt (Printers) Limited, 18/19 Delhi Street, St. Thomas, Swansea. Tel. (0792) 460913

The back cover of the programme for Wyndham Evans' testimonial match, Swansea City versus Liverpool.

Alan Curtis

My association with the Swans stretches back almost thirty years now, ever since I arrived at the club as a young trialist way back in 1971. I was in Porth Grammar School in the Rhondda Valley when I was invited down for a trial game by Mr Geoff Ford, the Swansea scout. The rest as they say is history.

I have been extremely fortunate in my career, both as a player and now currently as an assistant at the Swans. My playing career was a mixture of highs and lows, but thankfully the highs far outweighed the lows. The peak and highlight of my Swans career was that glorious ride from the old Fourth Division to the old First Division. There were some great games and I had the privilege of playing with some great players. I can remember drawing 4-4 with Rotherham Utd and Stockport County after being 1-4 and 0-4 behind respectively. And then there were other epic games like the promotion clinchers at Plymouth which we drew 2-2 and Halifax which we won 2-0. Another great night was the 2-1 win against Chesterfield, with John Toshack scoring a memorable winner. What a night that was, thousands upon thousands of Swans fans were there.

After a brief spell at Leeds Utd, the ride upwards continued in the Second Division. I marked my return with a penalty in a 1-0 win against our old rivals of the time, Watford. The last week of the 1981 season saw a tense thriller against Luton Town when we held out for a 2-2 draw before the magical 3-1 Preston party a few days later. That game and the following game against Leeds Utd, who we beat 5-1 at the start of the next season, are without doubt the two greatest matches I have ever played in.

It was the proudest time of my career to have played in what is now the Premiership in 1981/82. To have defeated the likes of Manchester Utd, Liverpool, Arsenal, Leeds Utd, Aston Villa, Man City and other great sides gave us all a massive thrill. Maybe the adventure lasted only too briefly, but the achievement will always be there, and if that was my highlight, then obviously the subsequent decline was the saddest part of my career.

We have drifted for many years, but there have been obvious exceptions – the Autoglass win of 1994 for instance. However, this new century brings much optimism. We are champions again, but you are only as good as your last result and we are pushing back the boundaries to get this great club back where it belongs. A new ground maybe too, great times are ahead.

Many thanks to Keith and Phil for giving me this opportunity to say a few words about the Swans, the team I love so dearly. I can assure you I share with you all the passion that you have for Swansea City, and will work as hard as I can as we push back towards football's elite.

Alan Curtis

Alan Curtis signs again for the Swans. His return was marked with the winning goal against old rivals Watford as the club rose to the very top of the football world.

Alan Curtis and Wyndham Evans, two great Swansea servants.

Jan Molby

Swansea City was my first managerial appointment. I was appointed by then chairman Doug Sharpe after being approached to work at Swansea by a consortium that were about to take over at the club. My first visit was in 1996, when Swansea City were fighting against relegation from the Second Division after a disappointing year of missed opportunities. They lost that day 1-0 but I felt the club needed stabilizing as a number of managers had been appointed and then sacked or left. It was a rocky time. That day at Swansea I watched them play Swindon Town and felt that I could do a job for the club. I left and a week or so later Doug Sharpe approached me, we met up at a service station of all places and the contract was signed. I threw myself in to getting the club in to a routine on and off the pitch. The players there were good enough I felt to stay up, my problem was we only had about fifteen games to get it right. I brought in Lee Chapman to help Steve Torpey up front and for a time it looked like we may just stay up. A run of wins against Walsall, Bristol City and Brentford gave us all hope, and the attendances shot up. But time was indeed against us, and even though we came close the club were relegated.

Our first season back in Division Three was crucial, we had to get back up. I had players there in Carl Heggs, Dai Thomas and Kwami Ampadu who would be instrumental in getting us promoted. Little Lee Jenkins was brought in and he looked a fine player, one for the future. For the majority of the season we remained in the top six, and I introduced Paul Brayson to the side from Newcastle Utd. He made a lot of difference. I even chipped in with six goals myself. One I remember well, a free kick against Peter Shilton which gave us a 1-0 win against Orient. I ran and ran across the front of the North Bank at Swansea, a sea of jubilant faces all reaching out and cheering. It was then I think I fell in love with the club and the area. These people deserved the success they had enjoyed only fifteen years previously. I was determined to succeed.

Throughout the season speculation was mounting that Doug Sharpe was about to sell the club. It affected the fans' morale, but we had one objective. We made it to the play-offs and defeated Chester City 3-0 on a warm May night in front of 10,000 Swansea fans – they sounded as if there were fifty thousand of them; it was very emotional. Our trip to Wembley was well planned. We had already beaten Northampton twice in the League and I saw no reason why we could not do it again. I know it's all history now, but I cannot describe the feeling I had when John Frain scored from a twice-taken free kick in the last minute. We had lost 1-0 and didn't even get a chance to get back into it. It was one of the most disappointing times in my football career. Those Swansea fans at Wembley were so upset and dejected it took me a long time to get over it.

In the summer Doug Sharpe did indeed leave Swansea and sold the club to new owners. The void we were in at this time whilst all the deals were being done meant we lost Carl Heggs, strangely enough to Northampton, and David Penney went to Cardiff, an unusual choice for a Swansea man. Steve Torpey also went for a good price in excess of £400,000 to Bristol City. With Steve Jones injured and maybe out of football forever the squad was looking depleted. It was always going to be hard. The new season in 1998 was indeed as hard as I thought, we gambled on players from the League of Wales, Tony Bird being one who I felt was good enough for this standard of football. But it wasn't meant to be for me, I parted company with the club after a miserable time and a game at Hull City which saw us lose 7-4 in one of the most absurd matches I had ever seen.

My time at Swansea was memorable. I wouldn't have changed a thing. The players there at the time were good people, they wanted the best for the club, but sometimes that isn't always enough. Maybe with more time Billy Ayre and I would have got it right, I felt my way of training and dealing with players was right, who can say what we might have achieved? People compared me to John Toshack, the Liverpool connection and all that, but I did things my way, the way I considered right. I always look for Swansea's results and wish the supporters of the club the very best. I had some great times with them. At dinners and sporting events I enjoyed their company and thank them all for their kindness and help whilst at Swansea. I have enjoyed the opportunity to speak to Keith about my time at the club. I wish you all the very best and will always have a place in my heart for the fans and will never forget the finest, most passionate voices I have ever heard belting out their praises from the North Bank for a fine club – Swansea City.

May you all get the success you deserve, and I will be cheering with you.

Jan Molby

I have enjoyed many a conversation with Jan, and always have a feeling of excitement when we speak on the phone or meet for a chat. He is inspiring. He is truly a 'good man' in all senses of those words, a fine footballer and a fine person. Swansea City were enriched as a club for his time there, and the fans, every last one of them I know would all like to say a big 'thank you' to Jan the Man, one of Swansea's most respected players and managers. Even in the twilight of his career his vision on the football field was superb – he was head and shoulders above his peers – and I wish him every success in the future as he proves to everyone just how good a manager he is.

Keith Haynes

David Gwyther

My Swansea playing career started way back in 1966 as a schoolboy with the club. Back then we were entering a bit of a down slope as a club, one which was going to take a good few years to get out of. Despite this, I enjoyed my spell there; it was a breeding ground for talent, even when times were hard. We had Herbie Williams and Mel Nurse there, two professionals in all senses of the word. Herbie, who I played up front with for many games, was a father figure to me. He would pick me up when I was down and point me in the right direction and this rubbed off on me when I moved on from the club and went to Rotherham, Halifax and later Newport County.

There are games of course that stand out – an FA Cup tie at Liverpool and again in the League Cup – but the most exhilarating game was at Leeds United in the FA Cup. I had scored to put the Swans 1-0 up and we seemed to be coasting to a result. Leeds with all their stars were getting nasty and Norman Hunter, Alan Clarke and all were putting it about which was meat and drink to Mel Nurse. Unfortunately Clarke spat at Mel and suffered the consequences… Sadly so did we, after Alan Clarke picked himself up Leeds equalised from the penalty spot. They went on to win 2-1, but Norman Hunter talks of it even now. I enjoy attending Mumbles Rangers end-of-season dinners and the one night I missed it (golf I'm afraid) Norman was the guest speaker. He recalled that game and the Swans side that ran the great Leeds team so close – they were top of the First Division and we were in the Fourth, but we gave them one hell of a game. We were a hard uncompromising side, as many will remember, and my style of play fitted in well with our tactics. I was top goalscorer for a number of seasons, hustling and bustling the goals in to the net, it really didn't matter how they went in, as long as they went in!

They were happy days at The Vetch Field. I scored a number of hat tricks, and remember taking Oxford for four goals one Saturday. Every time I scored it was a thrill, to score for your home town club was a wonderful feeling. The roving style of Herbie was good for us as a team and for me, it gave me lots of space and time. I left the club just before the golden years but have never taken my eye off the Swans' results and, of course, whenever I can, I'm at The Vetch Field. Where else would a man go for a football fix?

Swansea gave me international honours at Under-23 level, and I went on to be selected for the full squad too. Happy days, great days, and I will never forget them.

David Gwyther

Mike Lewis, Swansea City's General Manager for the new century.

An endorsement from Mike Lewis

I have been involved in Welsh football for many years. At Newport and Cardiff and now at this wonderful club, Swansea City. There is a proud tradition here, so proud that you can almost taste it at times. The fans are so passionate, and knowledgeable too, it is a breeding ground for real supporters of association football.

I came here many times in the eighties with Newport County before they sadly left the Football League. I remember the sad times at The Vetch Field, bankruptcy and near extinction – how familiar that felt when Newport left the world of football as we knew it then, and so soon after magnificent achievements in the European Cup Winners Cup. It just shows that nothing can be taken for granted these days.

I remember as a fresh faced commercial manager at Newport that most of the board had resigned. We installed a new chairman, Ron Warry. Not being totally happy with all footballing matters he asked me to find a new manager. I persuaded Colin Addison to come to Newport County after he had been sacked at Derby. I brought him along to the Vetch where we were playing the Swans in a mid-week Welsh Cup game. It was quite simply awful. Colin asked me to take him home after twenty minutes! Fortunately, Mr Warry did have the ability to sell fridges to Eskimos (he was a frozen foods man), Colin was talked round by Ron and the rest, as they say, is history. I also visited the Vetch when at Tottenham. I travelled down to Swansea with the Spurs team for a League Cup match. Ricardo Villa and Ossie Ardiles were with us then; I was looking after them. My task was to find them houses, carpets, all the things that make them happy and comfortable. That night my job was made even harder by one Tommy Smith who kicked poor Ossie all the way back to London. Ossie was nursing his hurt pride and various injuries on the way back. I asked him what he thought of Tommy Smith… the reply could not be repeated here.

But now I am a Jack, and happy to wave the Swansea flag.

We have here at Swansea so much to look up to. Wonderful players and characters, and nearly seventy international players who have played for the Swans. Now, with the ship steadied we look forward to greater things for the new century – great leadership and greater consequences of real achievement. We have that in place and I am proud to be a part of it. In Neil McClure we have an owner with bright ambition and solid business sense.

A great formula is being marshalled on the pitch too. John Hollins the manager whose name is on everyone's lips, and looking at these pages he knows exactly what he has to do to get the Swans in to the top flight again. He is a real professional.

I am happy to endorse this book, and feel humble when I read the memories of the Swans fans within it. Great days, great times, and I am sure there are many more ahead; just you wait and see.

Mike Lewis, General Manager

Acknowledgements

To all the fans and players that have contributed to this book, to the voices that have become words and the feelings that are now the written verse, we say 'thank you'.

Special thanks goes to Jon Wilsher at *The South Wales Evening Post*, George Edwards, James Howarth at Tempus Publishing, Mike Lewis at Swansea City FC, Gary Martin www. scfc.co.uk, Sporting Imprints, David Williams and of course Jan Molby, Wyndham Evans, Alan Curtis, Ian Walsh, Leighton James, Dave Gwyther and those visionary Swansea people of 1907 who made the dream a reality.

All reproductions of photographs and headlines from *The South Wales Daily Post* and *Evening Post* are with the kind permission of *The South Wales Evening Post*, courtesy of George Edwards. All other photographs are either owned by the individual contributor, Sporting Imprints or Sports Media Australia. Reproduction of these photographs and headlines must be applied for from the individual companies concerned.

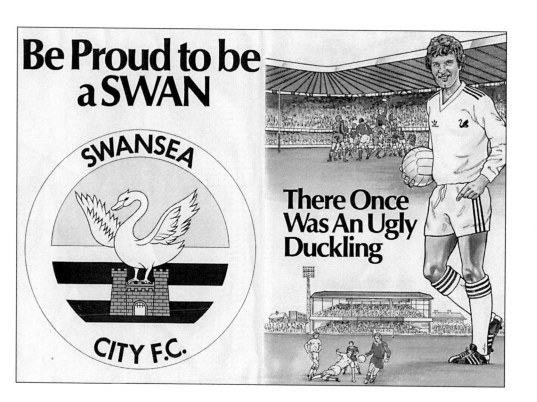

Also available from The History Press

Final Tie	Norman Shiel	0 7524 1669 3
The Football Programme	John Litster	0 7524 1855 6
Forever England	Mark Shaoul/Tony Williamson	0 7524 2042 9
Merthyr Tydfil FC	David Watkins	0 7524 1813 0
Newport County FC	Richard Shepherd	0 7524 1081 4
Swansea Town FC	Richard Shepherd	0 7524 1133 0
1966 World Cup Memories	Norman Shiel	0 7524 2045 3
Cardiff RFC	Duncan Gardiner/Alan Evans	0 7524 1608 1
The Five Nations Story	David Hands	0 7524 1851 3
Llanelli RFC	Bob Harragan	0 7524 1134 9
Newport RFC: 1874-1950	Steve Lewis	0 7524 1570 0
Glamorgan CCC	Andrew Hignell	0 7524 0792 9
Glamorgan CCC 2	Andrew Hignell	0 7524 1137 3
Glamorgan CCC 100 Greats	Andrew Hignell	0 7524 1879 3

For a full list of all our sports titles, please contact: Sales Department, The History Press, The Mill, Brimscombe Port, Stroud GL5 2QG; tel 01453 883300 or visit our website www.thehistorypress.co.uk.

Roger Freestone's Official Biography

Keith Haynes and Phil Sumbler have also worked together on *A Day at the Office: The Life and Times of Roger Freestone*. This is the story of Wales' number one, as told to the authors.

Keith Haynes has also written *Come on Cymru* and *Come on Cymru 2000!* If you would like to order these titles, or simply get in touch with Keith, send a sae to Ranto Yanto, PO Box 19, Gloucester GL3 4YA.

CHAPTER 1

In the Beginning

An attempt to run a good team

If all that is said is correct, something like a real attempt is to be made to run a good class association team at Swansea next season. Several prominent gentlemen are waiting to give their assistance, and this, added to the fact that there are several first class exponents of the dribbling code in the town, who have not played in local football, make it fairly certain that if an earnest attempt is made, a fair measure of success must come. The great difficulty of securing a ground, and in this connection it should be stated that in the event of an enclosure near Singleton not being secured, an application will be made to the Swansea Corporation for permission to get a playing pitch in one of the parks. If the team is formed, and there appears to be the possibility of good support, it is intended to join the Welsh Association. Many of the Swansea Town League players are said to be quite willing to throw in their lot with the new club.

Taken from The South Wales Daily Post,
Monday 6 May 1907.

First class team to be formed

Swansea is to have a first class soccer club next season. We have heard rumours of a professional team to be formed in the town of late. And the matter had been 'hanging fire' for so long that we almost gave up hope that anything would be done for the coming season. The delay, however, was not the fault of the promoters or the lack of enthusiasm, but solely on account of arranging sortable terms with The Gasworks Company for the lease of The Vetch Field. The matter of the ground was an all-important one, and The Vetch Field, on account of the area of accessibility was the ideal spot at which the committee who had the matter in hand concentrated. At last the obstacles have been overcome, and the public meeting held at The Royal Hotel on Friday evening Mr Thorpe (Chairman) told an interested audience that The Vetch Field could be leased for several years. He said that the 'Time was ripe' for a first class soccer club in the town. The rugby club were not supplying the class of football the spectators liked to see, and a good soccer club could give them much better entertainment. The object of this meeting was to see and discuss the availability of forming a soccer club in the town. Mr S.B. Williams, secretary of the Swansea League, commented upon the progress of the players and had 2,000 registered men for the soccer code. On the day of the Swansea v. London Harlequins rugby game he said there was a £50 gate at The Danygraig ground. This proved that soccer enthusiasts existed in Swansea. He contended there was room for both codes. He went on to say the Southern League could have a second division able to accommodate Swansea now that steps in Llanelly, Merthyr and even Cardiff had been made to establish soccer association clubs. The new Swansea club felt that they could accept the terms of the deal and pay the Gasworks such rent that would see soccer at The Vetch Field very soon. It would be a £75 fee for preliminary expenses and the profits would be determined at meetings in the future. Players would be coming to the town from as far as Aberdare, Merthyr and lands as far as Plymouth if this was to be a success.

Taken from The South Wales Daily Post,
Saturday 15 June, 1912

Swansea Town's New Manager

On Monday afternoon the directors and officials of Swansea Town Association Club held a meeting at the Cambrian Hotel for the purpose of appointing a manager. The applicants had previously been reduced to three. W. Whittikar (Exeter City, late Blackburn Rovers), Ben Hall (Derby County) and W. Annan (Bristol City) were interviewed. They having made the journey to Swansea at the invitation of the directors.

Eventually it was decided to appoint W. Whittikar as the player-manager. The appointment was made unanimously, and he will take up his duties on Monday next. Whittikar will keep goal for Swansea. He is a fine specimen of an athlete, being 6' 2" and 14st 8lb in attire. The signing on of new players takes place immediately.

Taken from The South Wales Daily Post,
Tuesday 16 July 1912

And so it had started. The club formed in 1912 as Swansea Town. Mr W. Whittikar would take care of affairs, and the club had secured a ground that would see them into the next century. Players would also come from as far as Merthyr too! The gentleman that had the ideas in 1907 and did indeed fulfil them as Swansea played as a separate club for the years before 1912 had pioneered a great historical event. Was the forming of a club in 1907 that was to inspire a professional club in 1912 to be Swansea's greatest historical event ever? Was it Swansea's most precious moment? They would never know. Their memories are left in the grounds of the club, yes, they are all dead now, finished and mainly forgotten – although not to everyone. But hail the men of Swansea from those times – they formed the club, they formed a lifetime of careers and dreams. In the Royal and Cambrian Hotels of the day the announcements were made. The players came, and graced the soccer code that was frowned upon from St Helens (the rugby club). They were gentlemen fond of the soccer code, gentlemen proud that soccer was to be their sport of choice. Picture them in their attire: bewhiskered businessmen, in full suited dress, all for the cause of soccer and its 'code', chewing over the relative assets of Whittikar, Hall and Annan. Whittikar, the man who kept goal for

Early Swansea Town action.

Exeter City being the winner and thus becoming the first Swansea Town player-manager of the twentieth century. Oh how I would have loved to have seen him in his attire keeping goal so athletically for Swansea Town. Of course no mention was made of ages in those days. No, it was not the done thing – suffice to say he was a man and an athletic, that would do. He was the first. There would be so many more to come, but he was the first and the club was born.

Vetch Field, Swansea

Saturday, 7th Sept. 1912

Southern League. Div. II.

CARDIFF CITY

v.

SWANSEA TOWN

KICK-OFF 3-30 P.M.

His Worship the Mayor has kindly
consented to kick-off.

ADMISSION 6d., BOYS 3d.

Entrances—William-st. Richardson-st
Season Ticket Coupon No. 1, Glamorgan-st

CHAPTER 2

The Best of Times

Where better a place to start than with those favourite memories? We will begin with Preston North End on Saturday 2 May 1981 when thousands of Swans fans ventured north. Swansea City won the game and clinched promotion to the old First Division. Like Wyndham said, it was a rollercoaster ride. Leighton James and Tommy Craig got the ball rolling in the first half then Preston got one back. But Jeremy Charles hammered home the third and the celebrating seemed to go on forever.

The sweetest sound of all

My favourite memory has to be the sound of the referee's whistle at Preston in 1981; it was the sweetest thing I have ever heard. I was overcome with joy and emotion – that type of day just stays with you forever and ever.

Clive Hughes, Coventry

C'mon you Blues

I will never forget that day in Preston in

1981. I was one of 12,000 Swans fans who had made the journey to Lancashire. It was just amazing, we won 3-1, Leighton James and Jeremy Charles being the crucial reason why we won that day. But my heart went out to all those Swans players, they played in blue, and Preston were just never in it. Unbelievable!

Huw Knight, Barnstaple, Devon

Pilgrimage to Preston

My dad drove us up to Preston; we left so early, it must have been six o' clock in the morning. I remember stopping at a service station, which was a real treat for us. As we got closer to Preston there seemed to thousands and thousands of Swansea City fans on buses and in cars. My dad said he had never seen anything like it before; I was ten at the time, and neither had I. We squeezed into the enclosure behind the goal and it was absolutely deafening. There were people with wigs and painted faces, gangs of lads with attitudes, coach parties of families and all to see Swansea try and

Swansea City reach the big-time – and in blue! Alan Curtis, Jeremy Charles and Robbie James celebrate the 3-1 footballing lesson given to Preston.

gain promotion to the First Division. When we did, my dad cried and cried. He was hanging off the fence at the side with his fist clenched, he looked so proud and happy. My brother lifted me onto his shoulders and we danced around the terraces singing 'Johnny Toshack's black and white army'. It was a very happy moment for me as a Swans fan, and now I am older I still get a tear in my eye when I think of my dad and what it meant to him.

James Thomas, Clydach, Swansea

A three day pilgrimage

Preston is a day I will never forget. Our car broke down on the way to the game and we were in a service station some ten miles from Preston at half-past two. The gearbox had fallen completely out of the car – we were holding it in with Tesco bags! We decided to hitch a lift to Preston, and of all the people to stop and give us a lift it was ex-Liverpool player, Ian Callaghan, he played for the Swans the season before. We got to the ground with minutes to spare and even though the whole day was a blur after that I will never forget Leighton James chipping the Preston 'keeper right in front of us. It took the six of us two days to get home, we travelled back to our home town of Haverfordwest at about ten miles an hour through 'B' roads and down via North Wales. When we did get home on the Monday morning my mother said 'Your tea is ruined, and your Aunty Megan has fallen down a big hole in the High Street'. To be honest with you, I couldn't care, we were in the top league for the first time.

Keith Haynes, Gloucester

How times change

Preston was amazing. The whole world lay at our feet after that game, and only six years after re-election to the Fourth Division and near bankruptcy. I just stood there at the end and cheered for so long my arms ached, as the players ran over to us and Tosh punched the air time and time again. I am not sure if anyone else could have got us this high, not even Harry Griffiths. Tosh was special, he knew what we had to do, and looking back now it was one of football's best achievements. It's true, the world seemed a better place when Swansea were in the First Division.

Phil Smith, Hereford

It must be destiny

I recall Swansea being tipped on the TV the night before to go up by Russell Grant when he professed to be an astrologer of some sort. He said 'For a certain team in West Wales, yes you are going up' – I will never forget that, and people can say what they want about astrology, there are certain things that are written, and it was written that Swansea City would be promoted.

Gavin Tait, Swansea

The best of times

I just dropped down on to my knees and cried at the final whistle. My mate John picked me up and shouted at me 'We've done it' over and over again. We just hugged and hugged and danced around

Swnasea City fans escort the team back to The Vetch Field.

with thousands of others for at least an hour. When we got back to our car someone had kicked the side of it and dented the door. It couldn't dampen our spirits, I opened the door, got in and slammed it shut. The dent in the door returned to normal. I think that just about sums up the day, nothing could go wrong. When we got home my wife told me she was pregnant with our son who is now an ardent Swans fan too. What a weekend!

Darren Reece, Llanelli

Wyndham told me

Like a lot of people I never went to Preston. I could say I did, but I just never went. I was desperate to find out the result and found a TV shop window in Cheltenham with pictures coming from Preston on the screens. It was *Grandstand*. I couldn't make out at first if we had won or not, and then I saw the beaming face of Wyndham Evans, I just knew we had won then. It was amazing, people must have worried about me as I cheered at a TV set in the middle of a Gloucestershire town on a Saturday evening. That achievement had never been equalled by any Swans team before that. Of all the people to tell me the news, it was Wyndham Evans, how many people can say that?

Jon Taylor, Gloucester

Celebrating in style

I just drank loads of beer and fell over.

Carl Steyton, Morriston, Swansea

John Toshack in pensive mood.

Happy days

It was one of my best memories, Preston v. Swansea at Deepdale. My lungs were bursting I sang so much, and the players danced with the fans after the game they were so jubilant. It was a fantastic day and it just makes you realise how much better it is to support a team like Swansea than, say, Manchester United. The winning tastes so much better when this happens.

Nigel Drean, Newport

Everyone wanted to be a part of it. Nigel Francis is in there somewhere.

Swansea are back!

We ran a bus from Swansea to Preston, and left on Thursday evening, you know, just in case there was traffic. Because we had quite a good run there we decided to go to a few pubs as it would have been rude not to. After all, they were open – and being a publican myself I have an affinity with other pub owners. We were in Preston by 9 p.m. A local asked me what we were doing there and I told him we were going to see Swansea get promotion to Division One. He said the game didn't start until Saturday! We all looked surprised and just stood there, the landlord was laughing so much and enjoyed our company to the extent where we stayed there until Saturday morning. The local just couldn't understand why we left so early but said 'I have never enjoyed myself so much in this pub before,' and I said to him, 'Now you know why we leave so early.' There was

a slight glint of understanding in his eyes… but only slight. We went straight back home after the game because one of the boys thought he had left the gas on.

David Spencer, Swansea

Numbing the pain

I was in hospital the day we got promoted to the old First Division. One of the nurses came to see me; I was in a groggy state after being sedated pre-op for appendicitis. I asked her how the Swans had got on. She told me they had won 3-1 and her husband had rang her from Preston to tell her. I was so happy. After the operation I was brought round and the first thing I said was 'Tell me it's true, the Swans won'. The nurse, who wasn't a football fan, just laughed at me. She then brought me loads of papers and a radio so I could listen to Radio Wales and all the after-match chat. I have been asked since if the operation hurt. The answer is no, I had the best anaesthetic money could buy – promotion – no pain at all. I made it to the promotion celebrations in the City though. I was in agony, I am pictured in a massive crowd walking along by the centre stands. The procession went on for miles: Swansea supporters for as far as the eye could see.

Nigel Francis, Dunvant

When Dad saw the light

My mother was a big Swans fan and took me and my sister to Preston by train. She loved football, and had been following the team for over thirty years. My father was more of a rugby sort, and rarely came to games with us. But this day he did come, and he was caught up in all the celebrations and promotion as much as anyone. So much so that for the next seven years, until he died, he was a season ticket holder at The Vetch Field. On the way home he told us that he never realised a game of football could be so tiring and enjoyable – it was probably only the fifth game he had seen. From that day on he never ridiculed football, and told everyone who did how much passion there was following Swansea City. Passion, he admitted, that never ever occurred at rugby games. That's the difference – I am sure the passion of the Swans support has won more games than other teams because of the noise and support they have when they run out on to the Vetch turf, and away from home they are magnificent.

Simon Keele, Carmarthen

Swans memories

The Swansea club were my life in the fifties and have been ever since. We used to travel by train to The Vetch Field from East Wales, through all the industry of the day. Hundreds of us all packed on the 11.20 train to Swansea from Newport. There was never a hint of trouble and Swansea were very well supported in the Cardiff area. The crowds Swansea Town got in those days were massive too. Everybody was just happy for a Welsh team to be playing such excellent fare; there was none of the nonsense you see today. That day in Preston was so emotional and overwhelming I couldn't stop crying for ages after the game. To think that John Toshack, a Cardiff-born man, could do that for a Swansea team just shows that Welsh football can be good again. I am now seventy-three and still think back to that wonderful day in Lancashire when we won the day 3-1. Illness and finances keep me away from the club more than in my youth, but I have my memories, and I still love to sit in the East Stand on matchdays and dream of all the wonderful memories and times I have had as a Swansea Town and now City fan. My wife and I dined out in Preston that night on scallops and oysters in a very posh restaurant. Some of the Preston players and their wives were there, they looked so gloomy. I raised my glass to them and toasted them. One of the players said to me that this particular Swansea side were the best team he had ever played against – I couldn't argue with him. They were the best Swansea team I had seen too. They were devilish and direct, and had so much flair and passion. Little was I to know at the time that an even better side was just around the corner. I am also a Cardiff man, but I have Swansea in my blood: it's horses for courses, it would be lovely to see both The Swans and Bluebirds in the top flight together. At least my Swans have been there in my lifetime, and I will never forget it.

Lloyd Thomas, Cardiff

Scoring that crucial goal

My memories of playing for the Swans are happy ones: under John Toshack we rose to the very top of the football world, that was some achievement. To play in a Welsh team that was the focus of the rest of the British Isles was wonderful. I remember well that day we travelled to Preston's ground in need of a victory to secure promotion. We were very confident – and you had to be, looking around the dressing room and seeing players like Jeremy Charles, Tommy Craig and the boss John Toshack all revelling in the day inspired me. We took to the pitch to a wall of noise from all around the ground, the whole place seemed to be full of Swans fans, it was a very touching moment. The game was good to play in, the sun was shining and the roar from the travelling Swansea fans spurred us on. I remember picking the ball up on the left-hand side of the pitch

Leighton James scores his crucial goal against Preston in 1981.

and moving towards the goal; there was still quite an angle to negotiate as I looked up. I decided to curl the ball round the Preston 'keeper, above his reach. I did so, and the ball was nestling in the back of the net and the terraces behind the goal and alongside me erupted. I recall being swamped by the players and the feeling is still indescribable. It was a fitting finale to a season we really didn't think would come right at one stage. We were in the middle of the table for a long time, and a run of victories at the end of the season took us in to the promotion places. A home win against Luton the week before would have made things easier, but we drew the game. However, no player would have swapped that day in Preston for anything. It was so fitting. The next season has to be the greatest in Swansea City's history – we took on and beat the very best that football had to offer. Beating Leeds United 5-1, Liverpool, Manchester United, Manchester City, West Ham, Arsenal, Southampton, – you name them, they came to The Vetch Field and we knocked them down. We even looked like we could win the League with a few games to go – imagine that, Swansea City as champions of the Premiership, because that's the equivalent today. I did move on after that, to Sunderland, but I am back in Wales now and working here. I always get to the Vetch whenever I can. Curt works there, that's brilliant to see a player who made the club great still there and moulding the future. I am a Swansea lad, a Swansea fan, and I make no bones about it. That's how much the club mean to me, and to be a part of the history of the place makes me very proud indeed.

Leighton James, Swansea City FC

CHAPTER 3

Favourite Players

There are so many of these for any team – more so at a club like Swansea. In one of the few club sides who have had players representing a whole country, the greats and the not-so-greats can easily become legends. That one moment, that one season or, in the case of some, a whole career makes all the difference to most of a nation. Amongst the ranks of Swansea players there have been Welsh internationals aplenty, English, Scottish and Irish too. When you go to a club like Swansea it quickly dawns on the players just how big the whole thing is with the concentrated journalism and the in-depth reporting not encountered in other so-called football areas. It sometimes makes the mind boggle just how concentrated the efforts of the press are in Wales. However, most of this list of Swansea stars are known nationally, and the reasons why are here for all to see.

Robbie James

Robbie James was my favourite. He was a bustling midfield dynamo, someone who you just knew would give his all for the shirt. He

dominated games at his height and caused many a defender's heart to flutter with good, hard challenges. A real Swansea boy, a real Swansea player, he epitomized everything about the team when he played – sheer class.

Glanville Anstey, Bristol

Ivor Allchurch

As a young Swans supporter I had the pleasure and good fortune to see Ivor Allchurch play for the Swans, he was absolute class, a real footballer.

Gary Martin, Llanelli

Super Roger

Roger Freestone is my all-time favourite. He is a class 'keeper, why he never made it at Chelsea is beyond me – in fact maybe he did, he seemed to play a lot of games for them. But when he came to Swansea he

A Swansea Town (Soccer Clubs)
bazooka sticker.

'BELL BOY' SERIES OF 72

famous SOCCER CLUBS

101

SWANSEA TOWN

FOOTBALL CLUB WAS FOUNDED ONLY IN 1911 ALTHOUGH SOCCER HAD BEEN PLAYED IN THIS RUGBY CONSCIOUS TOWN SINCE 1900. SWANSEA TOWN BECAME ONE OF THE ORIGINAL MEMBERS OF LEAGUE DIVISION III IN 1920. THE CLUB IS KNOWN POPULARLY AS "THE SWANS."

COLOURS·
SHIRTS: WHITE
SHORTS: WHITE
STOCKINGS: WHITE.
GROUND - VETCH FIELD, SWANSEA.
ANGLO-AMERICAN CHEWING GUM LTD HALIFAX ENGLAND.

was awesome: he is the ever-dependable 'keeper, good in the air, and takes the best penalty I have ever seen. There are a few outfield players who could take some tips from Roger. The fact he has set a goalkeeping record for clean sheets maybe proves my point, he is the best we have ever had.

Adrian John, Banbury

Bob Latchford

I thought Bob Latchford was the best, the very best; he was a goalscorer of immense class. His goals in the First Division when I was a young lad were memorable, he always seemed to score. I was only young, but I remember him scoring against a lot of the First Division teams of the early eighties. And he always had that excellent tight white Swans shirt of the time on, emblazoned with the black swan motif. That's my memory, of him turning away to the North Bank and celebrating another goal.

Jeremy Hubbard, Baglan Bay
(exiled in Cheltenham)

Wyndham Evans

Wyndham Evans was a brilliant servant to the club. A hard grafter and a strong

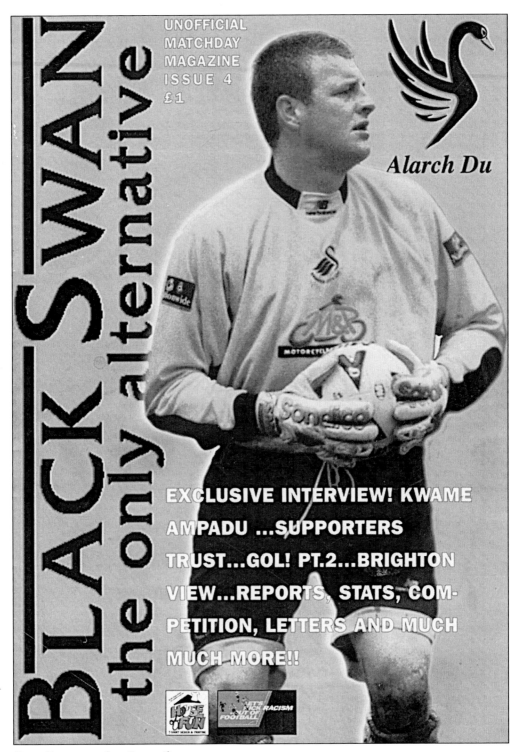

BLACK SWAN the only alternative

UNOFFICIAL MATCHDAY MAGAZINE ISSUE 4 £1

Alarch Du

EXCLUSIVE INTERVIEW! KWAME AMPADU ...SUPPORTERS TRUST...GOL! PT.2...BRIGHTON VIEW...REPORTS, STATS, COMPETITION, LETTERS AND MUCH MUCH MORE!!

Roger Freestone – best Swans 'keeper, ever.

Leighton James in action.

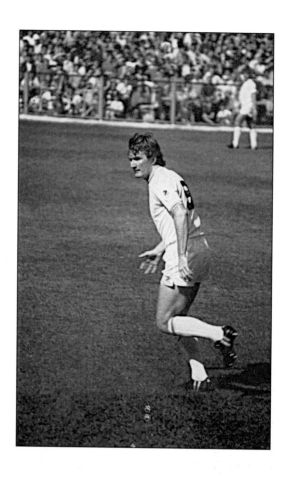

Leighton James

tackler, everyone knew they had been in a game when Wyndham was about. He was at the club so long I just took it for granted he would be there forever. He was never the most skilful of players, but his work rate was excellent and you just knew that Swansea City meant everything to him. What sums him up is the fact he was in the side in the Fourth Division and playing excellently and then he was captain when we were top of the First. I remember him being there when I first went to see the Swans play and he just stayed there – how many players do that these days?

Dave Naylor, Cirencester

My favourite has to be Leighton James; he was never equalled. He was a lightning winger, and he totally destroyed the First Division defences of 1981 and 1982. It was a sad day when we lost him to Sunderland, he had so much more to offer. He scored some crucial goals and was a controversial sort of player, I remember when we played Burnley and someone threw a meat pie at him because he used to play for them. That was Leighton, loved everywhere he went and then hated when he left. The reason why, though, is simple – he just tore the opposition apart.

Nigel Thomas, Swansea

Cyril Pearce

My favourite was Cyril Pearce, a real mobile striker, and someone who played because he loved to play. Back then – and this is over sixty years ago – you weren't the Fancy Dan of today. You played because you played, that was it. He scored 35 goals in one season back in the thirties. I remember him scoring a brilliant goal at The Vetch Field in the Welsh Cup final of 1932, a real individual effort that sunk Wrexham in front of a packed house. Maybe it's my old age talking, but I cannot compare the players of today with him, the closest we have had at Swansea would have been Bob Latchford, another real footballer who was a natural. If Cyril Pearce was playing today he would be worth more than Anelka and Cole put together, that's how good he was.

Arthur Tombs, Swansea

Cyril Pearce

It has to be Cyril Pearce. Back in the thirties my father used to take us to the Town field [Vetch Field] to see the Swansea club side play football. It was a depressing time for industry and we were in a recession, but he brightened up the day. There used to be a man who sold hot potatoes outside the ground and every week I saw him he would wink and say 'A hot potato means a goal for Cyril'. I think it's a bit of a sad thing that we have a mascot named after him – Cyril Pearce was a real footballer,

Cyril Pearce.

not a clown. I bought a lot of hot potatoes and saw a lot of Cyril's goals; if I could go back to those times and just marvel at some of the things he did, just for a moment, it would mean more to me than a lot of things we see today on the football pitch. I think his value would be multi-millions if we had him in a white shirt today.

Clive Owen, Swansea

Ivor Allchurch

Ivor Allchurch was a marvellous player, someone who genuinely wanted to play for Swansea Town. He was a Welsh international too, so a lot of people knew who Ivor was – a real great.

Jeff Thomas, Clydach, Swansea

Ivor Allchurch

No doubts about it, Ivor Allchurch. He was capped playing for The Swans at the age of twenty. I remember the game, it was against England on my birthday in 1950. He was an old-fashioned inside left, never shirked a tackle, always available and loved playing for us. He was one of a kind. The crowd loved him at Swansea, we used to sing 'I'm forever blowing bubbles' on the North Bank, and Ivor stood in front of us in a game one winter's day against Leicester City conducting the crowd. The Leicester players were laughing and applauded him afterwards. He never will be equalled – some of the prima donnas today would do well to look at Ivor as a role model.

Barry Simister, Swansea

A cigarette card of Ivor Allchurch, number 21 in the Famous Footballers series.

Ivor Allchurch

Ivor was magnificent, a real gentleman, very serious at times off the pitch, but that was his business. For me he would have walked in to the team of the early eighties with Tosh and all. In fact he would have been first on the team sheet.

Clive Roberts, Morriston, Swansea

A cigarette card of Terry Medwin, number 34 in the Famous Footballers series.

Medwin, Allchurch and Charles

Well, you look at players today and I wonder just where they are when compared to the likes of Terry Medwin and Ivor Allchurch. Terry was a true outside right, he was a leading goalscorer in the fifties and I was sorry to see him go to Spurs. He went about 1955 for a big fee, I think it was near £20,000. I saw him tear a number of quality international players apart in the red shirt of Wales too, for his country he was a real great – an old fashioned type of winger with pace and sharpness. Today he would be Ryan Giggs, that's how good Terry was. When he played for Wales the Swansea folk in the crowd always gave him a very good round of applause – no booing or anything like that. Even though the Swansea Town sides of the fifties rarely achieved real greatness the individual players were wonderful to watch. Big crowds, and lots of excitement, that's what these players brought to every game. The Swansea sides from 1950 to 1965 inspired people to go and watch them. We were always looking for honours, always revered by other clubs, and the players we produced have not been equalled in my opinion, with the exception of Alan Curtis and Robbie James. Local produce – that's what we were famed for, and remember John Charles played for the Swans as an amateur; who would do that today to get a foot in the door? It didn't do him any harm, did it? He went on to become the greatest ever Welshman at home and abroad, and it seemed unbelievable that he was once kicking a ball in Clarence Street with the young kids and then became the world's greatest football player for Juventus! No footballer is remembered like John Charles, a Swansea boy who led Juventus to greatness, beat that!

Colin Thomas, Burry Port

A cigarette card of John Charles, number 23 in the Famous Footballers series.

Jason Price

I like Jason Price the best. He is a good player. He stands out from the rest of the team because he is fast and scores good goals from a long way out. He also has a lot of skill and should be in the first team all the time.

Sarah Boyce, Haynes, Gloucester

Steve Jones

My favourite player is Steve Jones and I also like Jason Price. I like going to

Swansea, especially when there is a big game. I like the atmosphere best of all though.

Victoria Boyce, Haynes, Gloucester

Ivor Allchurch

Ivor Allchurch always had time for you. If he had a minute to spare it was for the fans. In those days you walked to the ground, as Ivor did. I can distinctly remember him walking down to the Vetch with his boots thrown over his back and a small bag under his arm. He used to come from the direction of Oxford Street, down to the ground, always say 'Hello'

and go in. Everybody knew who Ivor was, he was a real Swansea hero, but it was a different sort of admiration than today, a respectful admiration I would say. I remember him playing at Swansea at the start of his career and also at the end. He was getting on a bit in the 1960s when he came back, but he still looked a mark above the players we had at the time. I watched him at Haverfordwest after that, after I retired. He scored goals everywhere he went, but there was more to him than just that. He was a strong player and an honest player, he deserved all the plaudits he got of at the time. He was commented on as a 'gutsy man with silky skills' in a radio report before we played against England at Wembley. They would have

Vikki and ex-Chairman Steve Hamer at Swansea City versus Hull City, the last game of the 1998/99 season.

From left to right: Robbie James, John Toshack, Alan Curtis, Alan Waddle.

agreed afterwards, he destroyed them, and apparently England were the best there was at the time.

Derek Jenkins, Burry Port

Tommy Hutchinson

Tommy Hutchinson, easy, and he tops many a Coventry fan's all-time best player list too. He took on and destroyed Panathaniakos in a European Cup game at forty-three years of age. He was so committed and skilful, we rarely get players like him at any level – a born leader.

Steve Thomas, Coventry

John Toshack

John Toshack is my favourite just because of the things he did at Swansea. He scored so many goals when he came to the club, and he brought with him a load of really good players who complimented the youngsters we had.

Simon Roberts, Weston-super-Mare

The team of '81/82

Choose any one of the team that played for us in the First Division, the 1981/82 season. They played team football, unforgettable football.

Clive Hughes, Coventry

Dzemial Hadziabdic

Dzemial Hadziabdic was my all-time favourite player – the rapport he had with Leighton James was amazing. He came to Wales from Yugoslavia and set us alight, the spark we needed to get in to the First Division.

Stephen Richardson, Brentford

Roger Freestone

Roger Freestone – being a goalkeeper myself I appreciate the things he does. I would love to go training with him. He has been a real Swansea servant, and the best goalkeeper we have ever had.

Dai Davies, Port Tennant

Jeremy Charles

'Okay Charlo, now you're a Yagga Yagga!' What did that mean? Jeremy Charles was my favourite, sheer class. He totally tied up Martin O'Neil in a game against Norwich City in the First Division. I remember the look on O'Neil's face at the end – if only I could have captured that picture.

Pete Dempster, Carlisle

Jan Molby

Jan Molby was a superb passer of the ball – a real footballers' footballer. It's as simple as that really, he was a revelation at Swansea.

Ole Kamper, Naerum, Denmark

John Williams

My all-time favourite is John Williams. The flying postman they called him. He had great pace – won a fastest player in the League competition once – and he scored an amazing goal against Reading. He had all the attributes of a great player. He went to Coventry after leaving The Vetch Field and nearly played for England.

John Williams, Chiswick

Robbie James

You talk of favourites and you talk of Robbie James. What a great player he was. He scored so many great goals, and many from outside the area. I was disgusted when he came back to us, after serving football so well at Swansea and QPR, to be messed around with his contract. Even then he played his heart out for the club. The fans loved Robbie and it was such a shame that he died so young. My favourite memory of Robbie was when he was pulled down just outside the penalty area in the Second Division on the way up to the first. He went to put the ball on the penalty spot and the ref said it was only a free kick. Robbie shrugged his shoulders and placed the ball down about twenty yards out. The next thing it's in the back of the net. Robbie went over to the ref and pointed at the penalty spot, and then the place where he took the free kick from. I asked him later, at a dinner, what he said. He told me he told the ref it didn't really matter where the ball was, the end result was always going to be the same. I wondered why the ref was laughing. He was a great player, full

Jeremy Charles and Martin O'Neil at a packed Vetch Field. Note the rope in Charlo's back pocket.

of confidence, and lived life to the full, a barrel-chested man of great character, a real Swansea legend.

Martin Young, Swansea

Colin Pascoe

Colin Pascoe was my all time favourite, but my dad says Ivor Allchurch.

Barry Thomas, Cheltenham

Roger Freestone

I never saw Ivor Allchurch, so I reckon it has to be Roger Freestone. He has been a great servant to the club and rarely puts a foot (or hand) wrong. He should have played for Wales loads of times before now instead of some of the goalkeepers that have played for the national team.

Liam James, Trentham

Alan Curtis

No arguments at all, Alan Curtis was the man – that goal against Leeds United, and of course his goal of the season that day. The finest one-man performance I have ever seen, and that includes that lot from Manchester and all their so-called stars of today.

Len Lewis, Barry

John Cornforth

Now this may seem odd, but my favourite was John Cornforth – 'Super Johnny Cornforth' as we used to sing from the North Bank. It shouldn't surprise too many of the younger fans, except that I am fifty-five years of age. I reckon that JC could have played in the midfield of any of the great Swansea sides. He was a very composed player at his career's pinnacle, which we definitely saw at Swansea. My favourite goal was against Brentford in an away game in about 1993, a real rocket from a free kick. He scored plenty of others though and worked very well with Andy Legg. I was so proud of him when he lifted the Autoglass trophy in 1994, a real deserving captain who loved Swansea and should never have been allowed to leave. He always bought a drink for the fans and always said to me 'Lager tops

Alan Curtis, Swansea's best player ever?

Now, it's just ninety minutes to Wembley

Liverpool 1, Swansea 2　　　　　　　　**By HUGH JOHNS**

AS Swansea drove back over the hills into Wales early this St. David's Day morning, they were still toasting two Irishmen who yesterday played an outstanding role in putting a Welsh team only 90 minutes away from the twin towers of Wembley for the first time in 37 years.

Jimmy McLaughlin hit the rst and set up the second of Swansea's two goals which sensationally upset the Cup foreca sts. And Noel Dwyer darned near played the rugged Red Devils of Anfield on his own throughout the second half.

What an "L" of a week that was. First Liston, now Liverpool—two of the biggest "certs" in sporting history biting the dust. But Liverpool would have pulled off at least a draw but for Eire international Dwyer, who must be one of the greatest goalkeepers in Britain today,

The chilling, screaming, murderous Mersey Sound that belts from the Spion Kop raged round the Beatle haircut head of Dwyer throughout the entire second half.

But he was completely unnerved and made so many fantastic saves he almost silenced it.

Hundred of Swansea fans rushed out to mob him at the

A newspaper cutting that tells the story of Swansea's 2-1 victory over Liverpool in the 1964 FA Cup.

is it Dai?' He was a genuine Geordie who went on to play for Wales because of his grandfather's birthplace. It was a real bonus for all Swans fans to see him in a red shirt.

David Thomas, Port Tennant

Noel Dwyer

For one reason and one reason only I will say Noel Dwyer. He single-handedly kept Liverpool at bay during the FA Cup quarter-final at Anfield in 1964. We went on to beat Liverpool 2-1 and it was down to Noel, he was magnificent that day. I ran on the pitch afterwards (yes it happened then too) to congratulate Noel – he was a humble man, and said 'It was nothing'. If that was nothing then I would have hated to see him actually put himself out! He was a great goalkeeper for Swansea Town and has only been equalled by Jimmy Rimmer and Roger Freestone, but for one-off performances he

was the Jim Montgomery of 1964. It was quite simply incredible.

Trevor Banks, Swansea

Noel Dwyer

My favourite was Noel Dwyer, a great 'keeper, an agile man who kept goal for us in the mid-sixties. He easily makes it in to my all-time Swansea eleven.

Keith Davies, Gloucester

Alan Curtis

There are so many greats to choose from: Bob Latchford, who nearly won a cap for England whilst at Swansea, Leighton James who tore apart every side he played against and even John Cornforth, who captained the team when we won at Wembley. But my favourite has to be Alan Curtis, his goal against Leeds United from outside of the area in front of the Swansea North Bank in 1981 was incredible. He twisted and turned his way in to a good position before curling the ball around John Lukic. As he turned away and celebrated you could see what it meant to him – absolutely everything. The 24,000 in the ground that day went wild with excitement, and no wonder. It was an awesome goal. That day in the sunshine summed up Alan Curtis, a bright, shining player who loved Swansea City and the fans. He is a quiet man, unassuming and naturally mild in his manner, but he has inner qualities that made him a great Swansea player and an even better Welsh international. It's probably one of the reasons I would never like to see him as Swansea City manager. The next move for him would be the sack or to leave the club, and for Alan Curtis that would be tragic. He showed the real meaning of 'Swansea till I die' in the number eight shirt of Swansea City.

Keith Haynes, Gloucester

Ivor Allchurch

Ivor Allchurch had tremendous ball skills and vision. In the Swansea midfield he stood out from all the rest, and we had a good team then I can tell you. If only we had a Welsh midfielder with half his talent now.

Adrian O'Connor, Ruislip

David Giles

David Giles did it for me – he was a real pacy player, fast and cunning, with the ability to take on players. This was summed up for me in the FA Cup second replay against Crystal Palace at Ninian Park, in 1979 I think. There were 20,000 Swans fans there that night. He scored a real pressure goal from fifteen yards. Afterwards there was speculation he was on his way to every club in the country worth its salt. And I am not surprised; I travel about 60,000 miles in one season watching The Swans, and it's memories and occasions like this that make it all worthwhile.

Nick Rees, North Siberia, Russia

Tommy Hutchinson

Tommy Hutchinson used to inspire me, I remember him playing against Crewe and he was surrounded by four Crewe players. He back-kicked the ball, flicked it over their heads, ran on to it and set up a Swansea forward to score – of course he missed, but Tommy's range of skills were truly inspirational. I can see him now in that white 'DP' sponsored kit.

Keiron Mcdonnell, Peterborough

Jason Price

Jason Price, our current midfielder, is a real talent who hasn't yet played to the fullness of his ability. The reason for this is that he is played out of position too much. He scored a great goal against Millwall in the FA Cup in 1999 which helped us to win 3-0. I described it as a fantastic goal, and it was.

Laura Croft, Cardiff

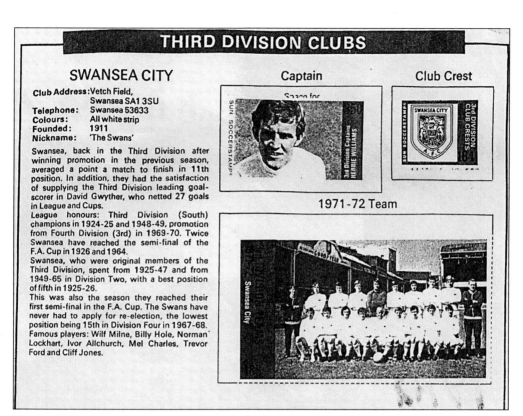

THIRD DIVISION CLUBS

SWANSEA CITY

Club Address: Vetch Field, Swansea SA1 3SU
Telephone: Swansea 53633
Colours: All white strip
Founded: 1911
Nickname: 'The Swans'

Swansea, back in the Third Division after winning promotion in the previous season, averaged a point a match to finish in 11th position. In addition, they had the satisfaction of supplying the Third Division leading goal-scorer in David Gwyther, who netted 27 goals in League and Cups.

League honours: Third Division (South) champions in 1924-25 and 1948-49, promotion from Fourth Division (3rd) in 1969-70. Twice Swansea have reached the semi-final of the F.A. Cup in 1926 and 1964.

Swansea, who were original members of the Third Division, spent from 1925-47 and from 1949-65 in Division Two, with a best position of fifth in 1925-26.

This was also the season they reached their first semi-final in the F.A. Cup. The Swans have never had to apply for re-election, the lowest position being 15th in Division Four in 1967-68.

Famous players: Wilf Milne, Billy Hole, Norman Lockhart, Ivor Allchurch, Mel Charles, Trevor Ford and Cliff Jones.

Captain

Club Crest

1971-72 Team

Swansea City. Just a few yards away from the birth of greatness.

Herbie Williams

Herbie Williams would get my vote as Swansea's finest player. He seemed to float in the air when the ball was coming near him. He would then meet it full on – a very strong player, and always a good bet to score.

Mike Morris, Ontario, Canada

Herbie Williams

Herbie Williams would make some howling mistakes, but he had to – he had to prove he was human some of the time. I used to try and emulate him: he had vision and took on players all the time. For a fairly tall man he had great skill, and the playground where I lived was full of Herbie-wannabes. In football terms he was my absolute favourite, the biz – never a great looking guy, but who cares, he was a Swan.

Cam, Brisbane, Australia

Robbie James

Robbie James could cross the ball from anywhere and he nearly always topped our goalscoring charts. He had great ability, and is a sad loss to the club. He would always do the unexpected and was a Swan through and through.

Ted Jones, Virginia, USA

Robbie James

Robbie James was my favourite player. I liked him so much I named my pet gerbil after him when I was a kid. I had two, the other one was called Alan, after Alan Curtis, another great player for the Swans.

Andy Fuge, Nottingham

Tommy Smith

Tommy Smith was a hard man, he was at the club with Ian Callaghan – both great Liverpool players. I remember Smith letting Ossie Ardiles know who was the boss when we played Tottenham in the League Cup: just kicked him and smiled. Ardiles didn't want to know after that. Of course it was one of those folklore cup ties. We drew at the Vetch and hammered them 3-1 at White Hart Lane. 'You should have heard the cockerel cry when the Swans scored number three!' Great days, made so much better by Smith and Callaghan in the white shirts of Swansea City.

David Knox, Llandovery

Ian Callaghan.

Tommy Smith, hard as nails – ask Ossie Ardiles.

CHAPTER 4

The Goals

Everyone has a favourite goal, be it the most significant or the most memorable (or maybe even just the funniest).

Max Thompson v. Arsenal, 1982

Max Thompson scoring against Arsenal in 1982. It was a screaming goal. My mate who is an Arsenal supporter was with me that day on the North Bank. He was gobsmacked! His face was a picture when Max's goal hit the back of the net – he stood out from everybody else purely by his facial expression.

Keith Davies, Gloucester

Max Thompson v. Arsenal, 1982

Max Thompson scoring against Arsenal was my favourite. It flew in to the net from thirty-odd yards, maybe more. The ground went mad, and we beat The Gunners quite easily that day.

Jeff Thomas, Clydach, Swansea

Jimmy Gilligan v. Cardiff City

Jimmy Gilligan's goal against Cardiff City in the FA Cup was the best goal for me. Usually I would go in the North Bank, but that day I got tickets in the East Stand and I was right behind him when it went in. The strike was from twenty-odd yards and flew into the centre of the goal – cue mass celebrations. Of course it was against Cardiff City so it was that much better – the strike was metaphorically like an arrow going straight through the heart of the baddie.

Paul Barret, West Cross, Swansea

Alan Curtis v. Leeds, 1981

Alan Curtis scoring against Leeds at the Vetch in August 1981, it was a brilliant day for us. 5-1 winners and on top of the League after the first day. We will never get back there so it stands out for me as the best goal we have ever scored.

Chris Wathan, Cardiff

Martin Thomas v. West Ham, 1999

Martin Thomas's goal against West Ham in the third round of the FA Cup in 1999 did it for me. The fact that West Ham were Premier League and we were Third Division at the time meant the goal was that much better. He just hit it and it swerved in to the net, leaving Hislop grasping at thin air. We won 1-0, so his goal clinched another scalp for us in a cracking cup run of a season.

Daniel Jones, Pontardawe

John Toshack v. Chesterfield

John Toshack's goal against Chesterfield in the Fourth Division set the standard that we were to keep for a number of seasons. That goal gave us all hope, and was the signal for years of success under him as a manager. His goal was a header, nothing classical just a proper goal, it showed us what we had been missing for a long time. It was the start of the rollercoaster ride we are all so familiar with at Swansea.

John Hughes, Tenby

Martin Thomas v. West Ham, 1999

Martin Thomas's goal against West Ham in the FA Cup was excellent. It was the first time a Third Division side had beaten a Premiership side in the FA Cup. It also meant more dreams of Wembley for us as we went into the fourth round.

James Howells, Eastleigh, Hampshire

Andy Legg v. Stoke

My favourite goal came in my favourite game. It was at the Vetch in Division Two against Stoke. This was during the 1991/92 season. Andy Legg scored the goal; it was a real long-range shot from the side of the pitch, and the fact he scored against Bruce Grobbelaar made it very special indeed. The atmosphere was special then too. Not many away fans come to Swansea, but Stoke brought a few with them, which whipped up the crowd. Andy's goal sent me potty – I had never seen a goal like it before.

Ian Wishart, Swansea

Jason Smith v. West Ham

Jason Smith against West Ham at Upton Park was a beautiful goal for lots of reasons. We had dominated the game and deserved the lead after loads of pressure. The atmosphere there was totally amazing, some 4,500 Swans fans cheering us on. I have been to many events – live rugby, Premiership football, and music concerts all over the place – but nothing has matched the atmosphere of that day. It gave me an enormous sense of pride to be a Swansea City fan being amongst all those passionate supporters. And Jason Smith took his header so well.

Chris Stevens, Dunvant, Swansea

John Hodge v. Bristol City, 1996

My favourite goal was John Hodge against Bristol City at The Vetch on a damp and cold night, the season we went down from the Second to the Third. Jan Molby had just taken over as manager and John was one of those players who thrived on someone like Molby. Although Molby didn't have enough time to keep us up, Hodgey rewarded us with a screamer from about thirty-five yards out. He collected the ball on the halfway line, nudged his way forward, looked up and belted it so hard the 'keeper was helpless. My mates and I just went mad. He was a favourite of mine and I was really sad when he left the club – he was a flair player, and we haven't had too many of them in recent times.

Karen Young, Gorseinon, Swansea

Martin Hayes v. Cardiff City, 1993

Martin Hayes was never a brilliant player for us, but he scored my favourite goal. It was against Cardiff City at Ninian Park in the Autoglass Trophy in 1993. It was live on Sky and the weather was awful. The crowd was decent – about 13,000 or so – and Martin Hayes scored in front of The Swans fans on the open terrace. The usual chants were flying about from the other lot so it was a real pleasure to (yet again) beat them on their own ground. They soon shut up when we scored the second goal. It was just a tap in, but the whole moment was special because it was against Cardiff City. I work in Cardiff, so I love every opportunity to take the rise out

of some of my colleagues – this was one of those times.

Ian Jones, Mount Pleasant, Swansea

Matthew Bound v. Cardiff City, 1998

Matthew Bounds' penalty against Cardiff City in 1998 was my best goal, for obvious reasons. It meant we won the game, but more importantly they had not beaten us in proper competition for years – they still haven't!

Robert Landers, Southgate, Swansea

Alan Curtis v. Leeds 1981

I was brought up on Swansea, my father used to take me, and now I go as often as I can. I remember sitting in The Garibaldi pub as an eight-year old before games. This started a ritual for me, and when 'Curt' slammed home that superb goal in 1981 against Leeds it crowned a superb day out. Curtis's skill, determination and endeavour made him a great player for Swansea City.

Jon Turner, Morriston, Swansea

Alan Curtis v. Southampton, 1982

Alan Curtis scored a wonderful goal on my eleventh birthday. It was April 13th 1982 against Southampton at The Vetch Field. My friend supported Southampton, so it was very special indeed. Curt scored some marvellous goals for Swansea and I was extremely upset as a youngster when he left the club. But that goal against Southampton seemed like miles outside the area, and it was a real flyer of a goal. Memorable for lots of reasons, one of the best birthday presents I had as a kid.

Phil Sumbler, Swansea

Before we start the next chapter let's take a look through the club's past. In 1925 the Swans won a Championship trophy for the first time. The date is Monday 4 May 1925 and a reporter from the local paper reflects and looks forward to the year 2000, anticipating a type of football that is state owned with all manner of inter-planetary competitions! He would not have known that the Swans team of 2000 would also be champions and would have been surprised to hear that the club still play at the Vetch Field. This is a humorous look at the views of a correspondent even further detached now than he was then.

Swansea Town and City have had three promotion sides that were to become Champions. First was the 1924/25 season, which produced Swansea Town's first ever championship, the Third Division (South) title. The Town side did it again at the end of the 1948/49 season. And, of course, as City the Swans dragged themselves to the top of Third Division at the climax of the 1999/2000 season. The most recent championship looked very unlikely in November 1999, with the team looking more likely to face a relegation battle than a championship win. However, like all Swansea sides that have won through and proved so many people wrong, they had more character than their rivals. Next are the headline makers of 1925, 1949 and 2000. Do not forget that whenever a Swans team wins a championship, records are broken. We never do things by halves.

FOOTBALL SPECIAL.

What To Expect In The Year 2000.

A GLANCE AHEAD.

**By L. V. MANNING
(Sporting Editor of the " Daily Sketch "
and " Illustrated Sunday Herald ").**

How he came to be in the room I don't pretend to be able to explain. All I know is that he was there, helping himself to my tobacco, and enjoying my whisky and soda like an ordinary mortal.

" It will be a great story," he said, " but I don't suppose they will believe me when I get back."

" Are you from abroad?" I gasped, when I had pulled myself together a little.

" In a sense," he admitted, " I am a journalist, and I have come a long way to see your football. We have heard some weird tales about your game in Mars, so the editor asked me to pop down and get a story, and—well, here we are."

He ignored my gasps of horror. Obviously, I was in the presence of a lunatic, or worse. My instinct was to dash for the door, but I realised he was nearer the exit than I, and I decided to humour him until help arrived.

" Tell me about it," I murmured coaxingly. " I'm awfully interested in Mars, really."

" Well, you see, our big season starts next month, and, as we are all out for the Inter-Planet Cup this time, we thought there might be a wrinkle or two to pick up down here.

THE FIRST ROUND.

" We meet Saturn in the first round," he added, " and if we can't slip some stunt over, we don't stand much chance. They are pretty good. You will remember what they did to Jupiter last—but perhaps you wouldn't," he broke off, to smile, pityingly. I let him go on. There wasn't much else to be done.

" It's extraordinarily quaint, your football. You are, I estimate, just about 850 years behind the civilised planets. There has been some talk of a challenge to your Football Association. We did in fact try to get in touch with you some years ago." (Those " signals " we read about in 1913 I thought!)

" Perhaps it is just as well we didn't succeed. It would have been very difficult to fix things up. You see, your game is so very different from ours. Many hundreds of years ago our football, according to documents found, was exactly like yours.

" The improvements began when the first Labour Government went into office. The Premier of those days—the celebrated Sir Ramsay McTillett—realised that, properly handled, football might be the most potent force on the planet. But, perhaps, you find this tedious," my mad Martian exclaimed.

" Go on," I begged. He was getting interesting.

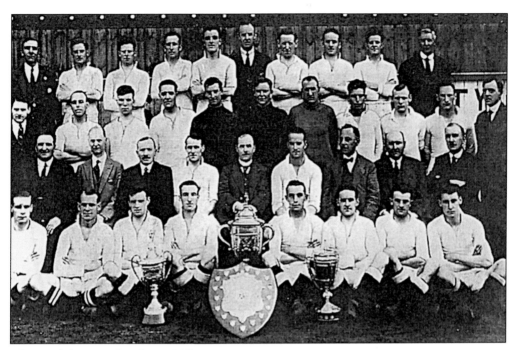

The squad that won the title in 1925.

The squad of 1949.

Press Opinions.

A Chorus of Praise for the Swans.

Below we publish some striking Press opinions:—

JOYOUS CLIMAX.

"Westminster Gazette."—The game was a joyous climax to a season full of hopes and fears, and they won fairly and squarely, reproducing all their old-time cleverness and dash.

SWANS TOO GOOD.

"Daily Herald."—The Exeter men did their best for Plymouth Argyle, and credit must be given them for doggedness and persistency, but the "Swans" were the cleverer side throughout.

SYKES' SKILL.

"Daily Chronicle."—Swansea not only deserved to win, but should have scored a more decisive success. The forwards were brilliant, and Sykes skippered the side with skill.

FURTHER PROMOTION NEXT YEAR.

"Western Mail."—It remains for Swansea Town now to build up the present very capable team, and the previous history of the club encourages the belief that nothing will be left undone to make further promotion next year a probability if not a certainty.

ALL WALES' CONGRATULATIONS.

"South Wales Argus,"—Well played, Swansea! All Wales will congratulate the Town on the successful conclusion to their gallant struggle to gain promotion from the Southern Section of the Third Division to the Second Division of the League. Their triumph has brought fresh honour to the Principality.

A PATIENT EFFORT.

"South Wales News."—It was a well-deserved success, the result of long training and patient effort, and gained after a hard struggle at the third attempt. It shows unmistakably that the advance of Soccer is not solely connected with Cardiff City, but is also marked in West Wales.

FOLLOWING CARDIFF CITY.

"Athletic News."—In the South, the Third Division promotion award has fallen to Swansea Town, so that Wales is still in the honours and has a representative hoping to follow in the footsteps of Cardiff City.

Press opinions of 1925 heralded a united Wales behind Swansea Town.

SWANS' SUCCESS IN GAME WITH BRISTOL CITY

By ROLANDE

SWANSEA TOWN .... 2; BRISTOL CITY 0

DESPITE a big effort by Bristol City to prevent them doing so, Swansea Town completed their home programme without a defeat, thus surpassing the record of the promotion team of twenty-five years ago.

It has been a great achievement, and the Swans can go forward to the Second Division confident that there are few better sides in the higher circle.

Their match with the City was patchy. For long periods the football was exceptionally good, both sides contributing many excellent phases, but there were other occasions when there were some very clear lapses.

WEAK FINISHING

In the main, however, it was a spectacular display, and the Swans did not find this last home game easy to win. Bristol City were weak in their finishing, as they were the previous Wednesday evening at Bristol, but they played well enough to call for the best in the Swans' defence, and this was supplied in good measure.

The match again served to bring to the front Elwell as the discovery of the season. In partnership with Keane he established a first-rate defence, and with such solidity behind the forwards were able to develop some impressive attacks, which were countered by another good defence from Stone and Bailey.

POLISHED HALVES

Edwards was an enterprising half-back, but no member of the City's middle line rose to the standard set by Paul, Weston and Burns, whose polished play emphasised the big part the middle line has played in winning promotion.

Scrine's header in 33 minutes from a Payne corner was a tonic at the right time, for the team went on to play very sound football, though it was not until the 80th minute that O'Driscoll got a second—a goal which took a lot of the life out of a City side which always had a chance of blotting Swansea's record while only a goal separating the sides.

Either Boxshall or Mullen might have scored for the City, but like the other forwards their finishing was very poor. The recall of Townsend was not a success, for he accomplished little against an immovable Weston. Teams:

SWANSEA TOWN—Canning; Elwell, Keane; Paul, Weston, Burns; O'Driscoll, McCrory, Scrine, Lucas, Payne.

BRISTOL CITY — Morgan; Stone, Bailey; Kearney, Roberts, Edwards; Boxshall, White, Townsend, Barney, Mullen.

Referee: Mr. E. Law West Bromwich.

Then there was 1949, when the records just kept on being broken.

The squad of 1999/2000 celebrate a magnificent victory at Rotherham in front of 2,500 travelling Swans fans and, of course, the Championship trophy. Records were set again, this time the record of best wins. Roger Freestone also celebrated the best-ever season for a Swansea goalkeeper, breaking the record number of clean sheets, set in 1949.

The fans just loved it – triumphant Swans supporters at Rotherham.

The seventies were a strange time. Swansea City went from bust to best, and half-way through the decade the club decided to wear a dragon on their chests instead of a Swan. They kept the white shirt, but surely no self-respecting Swansea fan would want anything other than a Swan on their kit.

The 1977/78 promotion squad. Back row; from left to right: James, Bartley, Bruton, Barber, J. Charles, Morris, Stevenson. Front row; from left to right: Moore, Chappell, Lally, Toshack, Evans, Curtis, T. James.

Record chase

Just one step from history!

By SPENCER FEENEY

SIX years ago Swansea City's season came to a miserable end with the Vetch Field club forced to seek re-election to the Football League after gathering a meagre 36 points from their 46 games to finis 91st out of the League's 92 clubs.

Tomorrow Swansea — the same in name but unrecognisable in spirit and achievement from the outfit of 1975 — will be one step away from joining the most demanding club company in the world.

Such is the measure of a success story that threatens to break all records

Since 1958-59, nobody has gone from the bottom rung to the top of the modern league as rapidly as Swansea are now poised to do.

Within two years of being re-elected, Swansea missed promotion under Harry griffiths' managership by one point, finishing fifth with 58 points in 1976-77.

The following season John Toshack arrived to take control, and the success story began with promotion from the Fourth Division.

It was an upward tale again the next season with Swansea climbing back to the Second Division they before.

After finishing 12 last season, they bid now to complete the story — at the same time breaking the record established by Northampton Town in the 1960s.

Ironically, the man who guided the East Midlands club to their finest period of success was Toshack's first international manager for Wales, Dave Bowen.

Under Bowen, Northampton's record read: 1960-61 — promoted Div. IV; '61-62—8th in Div. III; '62-63—champions of Div. III; '63-64—11th in Div. III; '64-65—promoted from Div. II.

As Northampton went up in 1965; so Swansea went down, relegated after an unbroken run in division two since winning the old Third Division South championship in 1948-49.

It would be nice to bring the circle fully around tomorrow

Let's not forget the golden era when the name of Swansea City was on the lips of every football fan. Here is a look at the headlines and memories of 1981 when the Swans were just one game away from the top division.

THE LIGHTING CENTRE

Lighting for all tastes

29 Oxford St., Swansea
Tel. 53401

South Wales Evening Post

LATE SPORTS FINAL

No. 33,567   SATURDAY, MAY 2, 1981   10p

Start-rite The Spring

SUNRAY

C, D, E and F fittings
£9.95

Grayne's

We are the Experts
42 The Kingsway, Swansea

Preston 1 . . . Swansea City 3

FIRST DIVISION

The headlines that said it all.

'Mission Impossible' reality for Swans

By PAUL CHAMBERT

THE impossible dream is today reality. Swansea City are in the First Division.

The nightmare, the humiliation and the ignominy of six years ago when the club languished at the bottom of the Fourth Division and had to plead for re-election to the Football League, is now a bad memory.

The record books will show that at 4.40 p.m. last Saturday, in the sunshine of Preston North End's historic Deepdale ground, Swansea City joined the elite of world soccer.

CHARISMATIC

The Swans had scraped into Division One by the skin of their teeth — but who cared? They were there.

Manager John Toshack — one of life's winners if ever there was one — and his team had achieved what many had thought was Mission Impossible.

And the charismatic Toshack — the latest of the Welsh Wizards — and hero of so many soccer campaigns, acknowledged along with thousands of other Swans

supporters: "It's the greatest day of my life."

For Swans chairman Mr. Malcolm Struel it was an ambition fulfilled.

It was a day that saw 10,000 of Tosh's black-and-white army streaming into Deepdale in a motley motorcade.

HUGGED

In the ground a formidable choir of Welsh voices swelled into a crescendo of Cwm Rhondda and the Welsh national anthem, exhortations to "Come on you Swans," and finally, when destiny was known, "We want Tosh."

At the final whistle, the track-suited Tosh ran on to the pitch and hugged his youngest player, Dudley Lewis.

He waved, blew kisses and threw his can of Coke into the heaving, chanting throng as he savoured yet another moment of glory, before doing a lap of honour.

In the dressing room, champagne corks popped amid the steam, sweat and back-slapping.

Mr. Struel, who had earlier joined his team on the pitch, said: "This is a day I've always dreamed about. I've achieved an ambition.

"We've been building for this day for six years. Getting into the First Division for us is like breaking the four-minute barrier for the mile in athletics.

"We live in an area that has felt the brunt of the recession and what we have achieved today will give Swansea and the whole Welsh nation a lift."

Assistant manager Terry Medwin said: "I left Swansea 25 years ago to play in the First Division and Alan Curtis did the same.

"Now we are both back home and

it's great. Players won't have to leave Swansea to play in Division One now."

The team, their wives, directors and staff, left for a celebratory dinner at a Liverpool hotel and arrived back in Swansea at 3 a.m. on Sunday to be met by a cheering 300-strong crowd.

● Crowdnote: Only 13 fans were arrested in Preston, eight from Swansea. They will appear in court to face charges under the Public Order Act, assault and drunkenness.

"One or two celebrating Swansea fans were arrested in Blackpool for minor things," said a Lancashire police spokesman.

Latchford the hat-trick hero

By JOHN BURGUM

SWANSEA CITY 5   LEEDS UTD. 1

BOB LATCHFORD struck a debut-making hat-trick in 10 minutes as Swansea City announced their First Division arrival with a performance of breathtaking quality against Leeds United at Vetch Field.

Leeds, very much in contention early on, were swept aside at the beginning of a second half which found stylish Swansea at their brilliant best.

Goalkeeper Dai Davies came through last night's reserve team friendly Pat Cardiff without aggravating a recent stomach strain and was preferred to Dave Stewart, missing his first League match since joining Swansea from West Brom 18 months ago.

Davies, signed for £45,000 from Wrexham, in the close season, joined two other summer recruits, defender Colin Irwin, Swansea's new skipper, and former Everton striker Bob Latchford.

Eddie Gray and Derek Parlane were both declared fit in a Leeds side containing England winger Peter Barnes, a £930,000 buy from West Brom, and former Nottingham Forest full-back Frank Gray, who rejoined the Elland Road club for £300,000.

Swansea's arrival in the First Division was marked by a reminder of last season's promotion campaign when manager John Toshack was presented with a gallon bottle of whisky for being nominated Manager of the Month for April. The action itself got underway in humid conditions with Swansea giving an early indication of their attacking adventure.

Swansea built a useful looking move down the left flank and when

● Turn to Back Page

● Turn to Back Page

VETCH FIELD LINE-UP

SWANSEA		LEEDS	
DAVIES	1	LUKIC	1
ROBINSON	2	HIRD	2
HADZIABDIC	3	GRAY (F.)	3
RAJKOVIC	4	FLYNN	4
IRWIN	5	HART	5
MAHONEY	6	CHERRY	6
CURTIS	7	HARRIS	7
JAMES (R.)	8	GRAHAM	8
JAMES (L.)	9	PARLANE	9
CHARLES	10	GRAY (E.)	10
LATCHFORD	11	BARNES	11
ATTLEY	Sub	STEVENSON	Sub

Referee: S. Bates, Bristol.

The remarkable victory that set alight the First Division in 1981 – Swansea City 5 Leeds United 1. The win included a Bob Latchford hat-trick and a goal of genuine quality from Curtis.

Curtis and Latchford celebrate the 5-1 drubbing of Leeds United on the opening day of the 1981/82 season.

A few years after those heady days came the sad news in 1985 that Swansea City were bankrupt. The South Wales Evening Post tells the sorry story.

Doug Sharpe earns a big place in Swansea history by assembling, provoking and eventually saving the club. The relief on everyone's face is clearly obvious.

Sean McCarthy sends the Swans on their way back to the Third Division.

The crowds have thinned out away from home but the die-hards are still there. Swans fans at Exeter as the 1990s get underway.

The 1994 squad that beat Huddersfield at Wembley in the Autoglass Trophy. It really doesn't matter what the competition is, it's there for the winning. A crowd of 50,000 watched the Swans win on penalties after a 1-1 extra-time draw.

Full circle back to the last Championship win.

Swansea fans at the Third Division decider away at Rotherham in 2000.

Hey, they can write too!

The fans flood onto the pitch to celebrate victory over Rotherham and winning the title.

CHAPTER 5

Up for the Cup

Let's pause for a minute and think about the FA Cup, The European Cup Winners Cup, the League Cup and, of course, the Welsh Cup. Swansea City have never won the FA Cup, they have never won a European Cup. Yes, they have won the Welsh Cup, on many occasions. Here we recall some of the Swans' most significant games in knock-out competition, both in the words of those who were there, and the headlines of the day.

Dancing in Monaco

I witnessed Swansea's record defeat at the hands of Monaco in 1991 – 8-0, oh why do we do it? The game for us was totally inconsequential, as we did the conga behind the goal in Monaco of all places! This had to be the biggest party atmosphere ever seen in an away end at a European game. The French TV director kept panning to the mad Jacks behind the goal as the party went on and the hapless Mark Kendall let in goal after goal. The French public must have been very confused indeed.

Howard Richmond, Bromsgrove

Music wins the day

One of my biggest disappointments was not making it to Villa Park for the FA Cup semi-final of 1964 versus Preston. Back then I was in a well-known band and we had a big gig on and I couldn't go. My brother went in my place and I had to make do with radio commentary of the game as we prepared for a prestigious night playing in London. We lost the game, and were so close to Wembley. Happily, nearly two decades later, the Preston story is a happier one.

Ron Griffiths, Hemel Hempstead

Hammering the Hammers

Beating West Ham in the FA Cup in 1999 was an amazing result – I live on it now, especially where I live. Never again will I get ribbed by West Ham fans about my support for Swansea City.

David Thomas, St Neots

Jason Smith heads home the first goal at Upton Park against West Ham in the third round of the 1998/99 FA Cup. The Swans beat the Hammers in the replay 1-0.

Short but sweet

Swansea City 1 West Ham 0 – I can't think of anything else to say.

Hugh Knight, Barnstaple

Oh lovejoy!

Taking the lead at Upton Park through Jason Smith, and teaching those lazy so-called stars at West Ham a lesson is a real cup memory I treasure. The passion and commitment shown by the Swans players and 4,000 fans that day beat the £40,000-a-week prima donnas into the ground.

James Catchpole, Lowestoft

Greek tragedy

Although we lost the game, I will never forget the 3-2 defeat at the Panathaniakos Olympic stadium in Greece in 1989. John Salako was playing for us then, and he was a real star. In the home tie we drew 3-3 in a pulsating game – these were real cup games. They really didn't deserve to

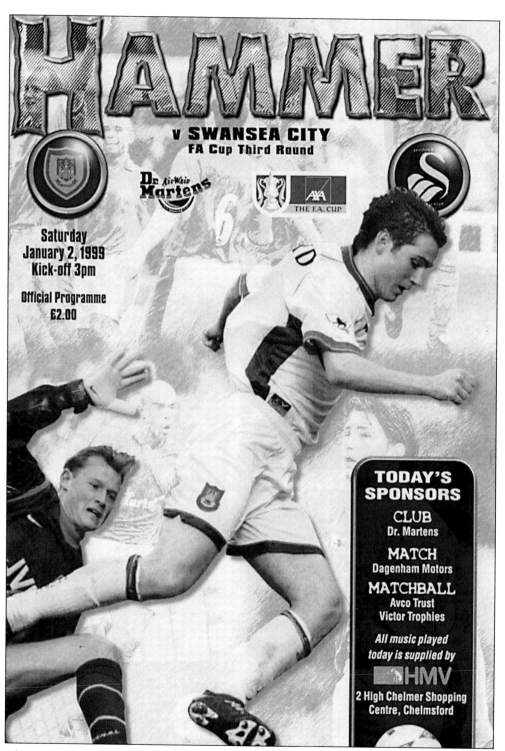

The programme for the 1998/99 FA Cup tie against West Ham.

win, but Swansea ran them to the end, quite literally. They got a very questionable penalty to get back into the game after Tommy Hutchinson had ripped then apart. We lost 6-5, but I am sure Panathaniakos will never forget us. They must have given the ref a few bob to get through that game, that's all I can say.

David Hughes, Newport

Let's all have a disco

What a game the Monaco away tie was – well for dancing anyway. We danced all through the game doing the conga. I went over with the TITS (The Independent Travelling Swans) and FOSCFA. We had a great few days away, and after fifteen minutes the result was totally insignificant!

Andy Lloyd, Gloucester

HTV Paris

I watched the Monaco game from a hotel room in the centre of Paris. I turned the TV on expecting a French news programme and watched the Swans in their yellow kit get demolished by Petit & Co. – 8-0. I recall laughing quite loudly, I think it could have been madness or the fact I never thought I would watch the Swans in Paris, on live TV in France, and not be there.

Jon Taylor, Gloucester

Feeling hot hot hot

Monaco is remembered for one reason only – the dancing behind the goal as George Weah ripped us apart and the Swans' goalie, Mark Kendall, conspired to let in eight goals, the majority of which should never have gone in. It was back in the days when you had to field a team of countrymen (not foreigners); in those days a foreigner was English as far as Swansea City (and pitiful UEFA) were concerned. We were doomed before we started – but the beer tasted quite nice…apparently.

Keith Haynes, Gloucester

The Swans v. the Swans

I was born in Walton, but my mother is from Swansea – and it was the only spur I needed to become a life-long Swans fan. My local club, Walton & Hersham FC, are also called the Swans and we played them in the FA Cup; the manager didn't even try to tap me up for some inside info either! In the fog and gloom the Swans beat my local side, and I was very proud indeed. Can you imagine the stick I would have got if we had lost the game? I never ever thought I would see Swansea City play at Stompond Lane, but they did and they did me proud.

Paul Arnold, Shedog, Isle of Arran

Better late than never

Bashley away in the FA Cup was a nightmare for me and the boys from Newcastle Emlyn and Lampeter. Our mini-bus broke down after a Severn Bridge detour – it was so windy the gateway was closed. So up around Gloucester we went and then due south to Hampshire. No way were we going to get there for the mid-day kick-off. The police told us the start had been delayed because a lot of the Swans support from Wales had been delayed – so we went for it. I watched the last five minutes, saw Torpey get the winner and off we went again for a long drive home. Ten hours in a mini-bus for five minutes of football! A cup classic? It may have been, I will never know.

Martin Piper, Wrexham

The Vicar of Vetchly

It's odd, after the FA Cup semi-final defeat at Villa Park to Preston in '64 my father, a minister in Mid-Wales, did a very strange thing – he swore! He muttered the words 'bugger' and 'damnation' in the same sentence and then just stared at me. Together we both laughed and it helped get over the absolute misery of defeat. My father was privileged to have seen the Swans team of 1926 beat Arsenal in the FA Cup quarter-final before going out again in the semi-final to Bolton. My father tells me that we lost 3-0 and the Bolton player who scored the winner in the final's surname was 'Jack' – enough to bring on another bout of swearing.

Hywel Thomas, Leeds

A real endorsement

Those Newcastle fans cheering 4,000 of us at St James Park in 1995. It was the FA Cup fourth round and we had beaten Middlesborough at Ayresome Park in the third round 2-1. We lost the game 3-0, but looked like we were going to do it at one point. Steve Torpey and Martin Hayes (yes the ex-Arsenal bloke) both missed sitters, then in the second half they hit us hard three times – 3-0 was the final result. The best result though was the affinity I felt with the Newcastle fans as we left the ground, they applauded us all the way back to the coaches.

David Naylor, Cirencester

Geordie Jack

I was born in Newcastle, and make no bones about it when asked. However, I am a Jack too, so when we played the Geordies in the cup in 1995, I was split down the middle. After the game I went into a bar with my black and white scarf tucked under my jacket. A fellow Geordie said that we had a good result. I replied 'did we?' – it was then that I realised that, although born in Newcastle, I was a Jack through and through. The Newcastle fan was astonished when I said I was a Swansea fan; we shared a few Newkies and off I was home – back to Swansea, where else?

Ged Thomas, Swansea

Noel Dwyer in action against Liverpool.

Liverpool rained shots on the Swansea Town goal in the 1964 FA Cup quarter-final, all to no avail. However, they won the FA Cup a year later by beating Leeds United in the final. In this shot, Dwyer is again in the thick of the action as Ronnie Whelan fires at goal.

Sitting ducks

I remember well that Swansea game at Anfield in 1964, we won 2-1. Noel Dwyer played the game of his life, talk about the luck of the Irish, we had it all. He was quite simply outstanding. We could have played all night and still have beaten the reds.

Neil Sinclair, Belfast

A bad tonic

We played Preston in the 1964 FA Cup semi-final at Villa Park. How many were there is beyond me – it was packed out, was it 68,000? I don't know, but the game was very nail-biting, we lost by the odd goal in three that day. After the magic of beating

Liverpool at Anfield, I really thought we had the cup wrapped up. Thousands of Swansea Town fans went home to Wales that night, most were very upset, you could see it written all over their faces. I was at University at the time in Birmingham and stayed away for a week, I couldn't face doing anything.

Carl Rogers, Cardiff

Villa Park nightmare

Villa Park was a nightmare come true. It was one of those games that you just knew we would lose after beating Liverpool, we were 1-0 up too. In the second half we folded – it was nerves and the fact we would be a Second Division club in a final that did it. A man next to me cried

73

SWANS DO A CUP CASSIUS!

- Swansea Town pulled off one of the biggest Cup shocks of all time with their 2—1 win at Liverpool. And the "Morris Minors," with only one other away victory this season, enter the semi-finals for the first time since 1926.

- Lancashire's hopes of an all Red-rose final were dashed. Though Preston pipped Oxford 2—1, Burnley crashed 2—3 at West Ham and Manchester United only drew 3—3.

- United were lucky to survive. They scored twice in the last four minutes and their first was an own goal from Sunderland centre-half Charlie Hurley.

Now, it's just ninety minutes to Wembley

Liverpool 1, Swansea 2

By HUGH JOHNS

AS Swansea drove back over the hills into Wales early this St. David's Day morning, they were still toasting two Irishmen who yesterday played an outstanding role in putting a Welsh team only 90 minutes away from the twin towers of Wembley for the first time in 37 years.

Jimmy McLaughlin hit the first and set up the second of Swansea's two goals which sensationally upset the Cup forecasts. And Noel Dwyer darned near played the rugged Red Devils of Anfield on his own throughout the second half. What an "L" of a week that was. First Liston, now Liverpool—two of the biggest "certs" in sporting history biting the dust. But Liverpool would have pulled off at least a draw but for Eire international Dwyer, who must be one of the greatest goalkeepers in Britain today.

The chilling, screaming, murderous Mersey Sound that belts from the Spion Kop raged round the Beatle haircut head of Dwyer throughout the entire second half.

But he was completely unnerved and made as many fantastic saves he almost silenced it.

Hundred of Swansea fans rushed out to kiss him at the final whistle and even the saddened Kop fans gave him a silver as he rushed off.

They'd seen an incredible point-blank save from Callaghan, two more from Hunt, which seemed incredible—and, even when lying flat on his back, Dwyer once managed to twist and out-hand a biting "certainty" off the line.

Penalty miss

So unfortunate did he seem that Ron Moran gave a penalty that would have handed a replay high into the Kop crowd trying over-hand to place his shot out of Dwyer's reach.

Dwyer was beaten only twice, both times by Liverpool's outstanding player, Peter Thompson. One shot hit the post and the other narrowed Swansea's lead.

CARDIFF SAG AS WILLIAMS IS SENT OFF

By Brian Eastham

HUDDERSFIELD 1, CARDIFF 1

ONLY John Charlie kept a level head when injured Cardiff man suffered by Huddersfield pressure in the second half.

Cardiff right-half Gareth Williams was sent off after an incident involving Huddersfield centre-forward Stokes.

Huddersfield at the same time were awarded a penalty, which Les Massie for inside-right kicked. This equalised Cardiff's earlier goal by Scott.

Huddersfield 'keeper trying to collect a long throughpass, was bowled over and while he was lying dazed, Scott slipped the ball into the net.

Most of the Cardiff team plundered round referee Faulkner's protesting against the sending off of Williams. Cardiff afterwards went to pieces. Their rushes were easily checked by the Huddersfield defenders.

Near time, Huddersfield sneaked the points with a smartly taken goal at centre-forward Stokes, whose duel with John Charles was one of the brightest features of this lively match, which was starred only by Cardiff's lack of aggression.

Huddersfield introduced inside-right half-winger Fraser.

This first game was a one for Fraser but he should have a victory fixture in League football. His accurate centres were always a threat to the Cardiff defence.

HUDDERSFIELD.— Wood; Coddington, Atkins; R. Wilson 1; Coen 1, Meagan; Scanlon, Massie 1, Stokes 1, McHale, Fraser.

CARDIFF.— Dilwyn John; Harrington, Milne; Hole; King 1, Quinn; Lea, Charles (W.), King 1, Tapscott, Farrell (Liverpool) 1.

● WHAT A HOPE! Liverpool forward Roger Hunt scarcely gets a look in as Swansea's triumphant defence goes into action—Brian Purcell (5), Herbie Williams (6) and 'keeper Noel Dwyer soar together to a cross from winger Callaghan.

BYRNE'S TOO HOT FOR DOUBLE-STOPPER PLAN

By RALPH HADLEY

West Ham 3, Burnley 2

Argyle hit

How the national papers saw the win over Liverpool.

The scene of one of Swansea'a most important games ever – Villa Park.

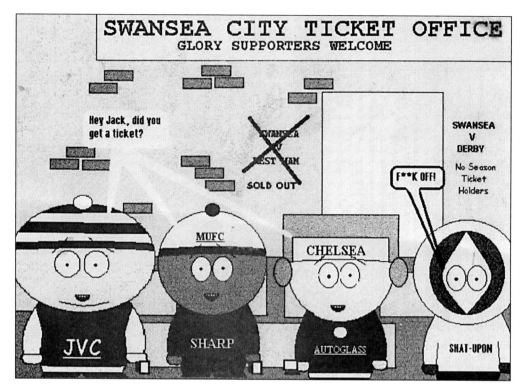

A cover from Jackanory *covering the fine FA Cup exploits of 1998/99.*

for ages at the final whistle; it was one of those games you never forget.

Andrew Manton, Swansea

Wembley dreams

Winning the Autoglass Trophy at Wembley was a memorable moment for me. John Cornforth lifting that trophy was a memory I will never forget.

Dave Hayes, Bristol

Everyone loves an underdog

The FA cup run of 1998/99 was a superb boost for the Swans' support and for the club financially too. The main memory has to that of Martin Thomas bending in that winner at The Vetch on a cold winter's night and lying down in front of The North Bank as it rocked in celebration. The other has to be Roger Freestone's superb save to keep Neil Ruddock out at the end: now that was real cup-tie stuff. On my way to work the next day a bloke got out of his car and ran up to me. He had seen a Swansea sticker in the back window of my car. He just kept shaking my hand and saying 'Well done mate, well done'.

Keith Haynes, Gloucester

Crowning triumph – How the Swans won the cup – A thrilling final (Stewart Hall, eat your heart out).

For the first time in its long history the Swans have won the Welsh Cup. On Thursday evening amid unprecedented scenes the Swans did it. The train came in to Swansea from Tonypandy and the Swans fans were in great voice. All approaches to the station were packed with people. One vast sea of faces extending from the town end of The New Cut Bridge cheered for hours. My head aches even now. A brake was in waiting to carry the team to the Royal Hotel, but long before the team arrived the crowd had affixed the horses and had attached ropes from the shaft. Jock Hamilton the skipper and Mr Thorpe the Chairman were given ovations as each of the team came in to view. The first season of football had brought a cup to the town. A band was in attendance and a few score or more paraded up and down with vigour. They were harnessed to the brake. The King himself could not have had a more enthusiastic welcome. The procession went through Wind Street, on to Castle Street and then High Street. King Football was here. Jock Hamilton, cup in hand attempted to address the crowd, but they could not hear for the cheering. He was later more successful from the balcony of the Royal Hotel. 'I have no doubt you are as delighted as I am' he shouted. 'What a grand sport our Jock is' determined Mr Thorpe. 'I am pleased to receive such a trophy for the club he said. The talk was of a first national cup to ever be brought to Swansea, fixed looks stated they knew not of another time or occasion. As the crowd swelled and songs of victory floated the night away I sat perplexed on my horse and wondered. Was I here for a reason? I could not answer but put forward my notes for you to consider. A great win at Tonypandy, and I a man of mere kindness to witness the long journey home. Hail the soccer club for I am a part of it.

A report by 'Ajax' from the South Wales Daily, *Friday 25 April 1913*

Swans in Pontypridd Welsh Cup win

Swansea soccer is here. The mud of the pitch and the excitement of the crowd gave Swansea the victory. The team made the pitch look perfect though their legs were deep in mud for some time. They were the only team capable of perfect Association Football. The Pontypridd Dragons were being well and truly beaten. At last the ball fell to Duffy and his right half did not part, the ball was placed to Messer who ran on and stung out a shot – bang went the ball straight for the net. The ball fell short, and Grierson with splendid position and followed by a scene of unprecedented enthusiasm placed the ball into the net. The Swans worked at their play throughout, they were the leather winners of the day, and the team as one are to be honoured. A great cup win.

The South Wales Daily Post, *extra special Friday 25 April 1913*

Family ties

My grandfather was a town councillor in 1913 and before he died in 1968 he told me of the day the Swans won the cup of Wales for the first time. He talked of massive crowds in Swansea and recalled choruses of singing in the town centre for much of the night. He was not a football man until then, rugby being the code he preferred, but after the Welsh Cup win he never looked to the rugby ball again. Nowadays I get to the Vetch as often as I can, it's traditional. In quieter moments I reflect on what it must have been like all those years ago when football was new to Swansea. The talk of moving to a new ground sometimes annoys me, we have so many cherished memories at Swansea and being at The Vetch. Those pioneers of football back then were strong men – they had to be to take on the closed ranks of the Welsh rugby world.

Jeff Thomas, Townhill, Swansea

Continental clashes

I remember Locomotive Leipzig in the European Cup Winners Cup: they took sportsmanship to a new level – cheating I think I called it. They contrived to fall over all night and sneaked a goal right at the end; talk about a liberty! And then there's those heady days of taking on Paris St Germain in the early eighties; so near and yet so far. The most treasured memory I have is the defeat of Red Star Belgrade in a pre-season friendly at The Vetch Field. We must have put eight goals past them before they realized where they were.

Howard Richmond, Bromsgrove

Malteesered!

Sliema Wanderers, that was one fantastic

night. 12-0 we beat them in the European Cup Winners Cup. Ian Walsh scored five I think! The away leg was never in doubt, we struggled to a 5-0 win if my memory serves me right.

Gary Anderson, Swansea

5-0

The most amazing cup game I ever saw at The Vetch Field was around about 1980 or so. We played Middlesbrough in the FA Cup. They had five attacks and beat us 5-0. I was stunned. The manager of Boro said at the time he just couldn't see how we had not beaten them. We were all over them for the whole game – incredible.

Dave Earnshaw, Caldicot

Vive la France

I went to Paris for the second leg of the game against Paris SG. They were leading from the first leg by the odd goal or so and I really didn't expect us to win. I travelled with a load of boys from Swansea by coach, and by the time we got to Cardiff we were all well on the way in the drinking stakes. I was the only one who had been to France before so I became the tour guide for the day. We visited all the red light areas and lost a few on the way. We then went on to the game. We lost, not by much though, and it took three days to get back home, something distracted us in Paris, but I'm not saying what it was.

Ian Williams, Clydach, Swansea

Nice ice cold milk

We brought back a guy from Paris with us who had been over there for some time. He turned up at the game wearing a huge daffodil and had no shoes on. He had stayed over there after a rugby international and wanted a lift home. He had been through quite a rough time by all accounts. He stood there amongst two thousand or so Swans fans asking for a lift home. We took pity on him and offered him a lift back. He wrote to all of us afterwards and sent us a tenner each for being so kind. I saw him ten years or so later when I started work at the milk factory in Whitland – he was my supervisor. Time off was never a problem for me.

Gerry Thomas, Haverfordwest

CHAPTER 6

Reasons to be a Jack

Why do people support Swansea City? After all, they are not the most glamorous of clubs and the trophy cabinet is hardly brimming over with silverware. However, Swansea supporters are vocal, passionate and very proud of their team and their Welsh heritage. For me, it started as a kid in 1978 on a Saturday afternoon when my elder brother informed me that the Swans had won and a love affair was born. Here we look at the reasons why some Swansea supporters choose the black and white shirt.

Remember the first time

My first experience of Swansea City was attending the Vetch with my father when I was a young boy. When John Toshack came to Swansea City I was eight, and I realised that he was building a team that believed it could beat anyone, playing football the way it was meant to be played.

Gary Elsey, Gorseinon, Swansea

More of a vocation really

Let's face it, Swansea City are not the world's most glamorous team so I can only presume that there was some form of spiritual call that first led me to The Vetch. There can't be any other explanation!

Paul Barrett, West Cross, Swansea

What will be

I started supporting the Swans in 1958 – a ten-year old kid from Carmarthen. Before that, I'd always look in the paper for the scores etc, but I never attended a game until I was ten – mainly because no-one would take me on the packed-lunch journey to the big city! My dad worked most Saturdays, and he preferred rugby anyway. Eventually, after much nagging and manipulating, at least in kid terms, I was allowed to go to a game with one of my mates.

Cam, Brisbane, Australia

It feels like home

There must be Swansea City in my blood. The Vetch Field has too many of my hopes, dreams and memories tied up in it for me to ever think about leaving them as my team.

Andy Williams, Porthcawl

Keep it in the family

I was born and bred in Swansea. I was first taken to the Vetch by my dad when I was nine and have been hooked since. I moved away in 1983 and, as a result, I am now more proud of my roots. Supporting Swansea is a big part of who I am and where I'm from.

Andy Fuge, Nottingham

Match of the day

The highlight of my week when I was younger was staying with my gran, who lived on St Helens Avenue, and being able to watch the Swans every other week. I love the atmosphere that is created at the Vetch and the city in general.

Mark James, Southampton, Bermuda

You can't beat the real thing

My uncle first took me to the Vetch when they were in the old Fourth Division. I fell in love with the idea of watching 'real' people play football as opposed to just seeing it on television.

Matthew Parsell, Aberdare

The Danish connection

I first saw Swansea at Wembley in 1997 and got to know a few of the players as well as fellow Dane, Jan Molby. I came back the following year and was well treated by all at the Vetch. Liverpool had always been my club, but I started following Swansea when Toshack was appointed as manager. Thanks to the internet, I can now keep in touch with life at Swansea, despite living many miles away.

Ole Kamper, Naerum, Denmark

I think I love you

I was born and bought up in Bethesda, Gwynedd, and as a child I followed the local team – Bethesda Athletic. I did also want to support a big club and chose Leeds United at first as I'd seen them win the 1967 League Cup. They also played in a white strip, which I always associated with the great Real Madrid team of the 1960s. Leeds' main rivals at the time were Liverpool, who had John Toshack in the team. So although I always wanted Leeds to win, I was always pleased when Toshack played well and scored. In the late 1970s I moved to live in Mumbles which coincided with Toshack's move to the Vetch. As in other places I had lived, I was a lover of football and attended the Vetch for a Fourth Division match. I can't remember the opposition – that wasn't important – but what I do remember was falling in love with the Swans. To me, they had everything, they were a good team, a 'big' team, they were Welsh, they had heroes such as Waddle and Tosh as manager, a passionate crowd and they played in white! To me, these factors put them on a different plane and from that day forward, my love affair with the Swans had begun.

John Hughes, Tenby

Like father like son

My father was a season-ticket holder at the Vetch when I was younger and he took me along; it was almost as if I was born to be a Swansea City supporter. I have so many memories of Swansea City from my childhood in my mind – I guess I have never looked back from that first visit as a youngster!

Jon Turner, Morriston, Swansea

Through thick and thin

I have seen Swansea in my time at the very top of the old First Division and at the bottom of the old Fourth Division. They are my local team and I will always support them no matter where they are playing. When I can't get to see them in action for whatever reason, I am always desperate to find out how they are getting on.

Chris Stevens, Dunvant, Swansea

No other option would do

I love my hometown of Swansea and I love football. It was only natural that I would follow Swansea therefore, as Swansea City is the one medium that combines both of these two elements.

Chris Ollier, Dunvant, Swansea

Common sense

It used to annoy me that some of my friends would support a 'glamour' club such as Liverpool, who, at the time, won just about everything in sight. I didn't want any of that for my football allegiance and therefore I turned to my local club in Swansea. To me that makes me a 'real' football supporter that stands out in the crowd!

Mark Goddard, Llanelli

Swansea City – pride of Wales

I have no idea why I support Swansea! Seriously, they are my local League club and I've been a fan for twenty-three years. Cardiff are classed as Wales' premier club, and I would dearly love to prove to everyone that in reality this title should be bestowed on Swansea City. I could go on all day about the reasons but there has never been anyone else.

Mike Davies, London

Just the tonic

I've been attending the Vetch since my dad took me when I was just a little Jack in the making. A Saturday afternoon would not be the same without my weekly dose of Swansea City.

Daniel Jones, Pontardawe, Swansea

Where the heart is

Nobody I know in Pembrokeshire supports any other team except Swansea City. I have

The sheer joy of being a Swansea fan; travelling Swans at Plymouth as Toshack gets the ball rolling.

never ever seen a Cardiff City fan down here, not ever. I heard once there was one in Pembroke Dock, but I reckon it was a wind up.

Paul Thomas, Haverfordwest

A tough call

It would have been easy for me to start supporting a 'big' team such as Manchester United or Arsenal, but I plumped in the end for Swansea City. I don't believe that

there is another ground within the English leagues that can recreate the atmosphere that is generated at the Vetch when the Swans are at home.

Jenny Milligan, Peterborough

All aboard

Swansea City are so unpredictable – you never know what is going to happen next. One week you are being thrashed at Exeter and the next week outclassing Premiership opposition. It's a real roller-coaster ride as a Swansea fan.

Tim Jones, Dunvant, Swansea

No mistake

I was first taken to the Vetch in 1983. At first I guess it was the 'wall of sound' that attracted me – several thousand voices blended into one – but now I would have to say hometown pride is the main reason.

Keiron McDonnell, Peterborough

To even think of changing my team!

I can imagine it now, my father would kill me. I had no choice, I was a Swans fan from the age of two months, taken to games, pictured in the programme, everything. There was no way I could support anyone else. It wasn't allowed!

Martin Levy, Chepstow

From everywhere

John Toshack was my hero. When he went to Swansea I followed them and have done ever since. It's surprising really just how many Swans fans live in the capital city, I have regularly travelled to games with a group of Swans supporters for the past twenty-five years from Cardiff. There have been times when the majority of a train from Cardiff to Swansea has been full of Swans fans from the area.

John Rice, Pencoed

The national pastime

How can you be Welsh and not a Swans fan? I have travelled from Brecon to the Vetch over a thousand times in my lifetime – ever since the days of Ivor Allchurch and the Hole brothers. The support up in Brecon is split between Cardiff and Swansea, but remember this is an area where it is just as easy to get to Birmingham and Bristol as it is to Swansea. I couldn't imagine being anything else other than a Swansea fan.

Bryn Lane, Brecon

Family ties

I have followed the fortunes of Swansea as a Town and City football side for sixty-odd years. My father was employed by the club and spent the week at the Vetch in the forties, and travelled home on Sundays for two days off. The train journey took three hours from Milford then.

Winifred Thomas, Milford Haven

Institutionalized

My Uncle Keith took me to my first game in 1997, it was against Northampton and we won 2-1. I was also at Wembley when we lost. I love following Swansea and always look out for their results. I have got some Swansea kits too, which I wear to school – all the people in my class support Man United or Liverpool, but I don't.

Lee Haynes, Northampton

Simon and Speedy pose for the camera.

Man and boy

I have supported the Swans ever since I was a child. I was a ball boy when I was eight years of age, and have pictures of me with Nigel Stevenson. I was at Trebanos AFC at the time – it was 1982/83 – and he presented me with a medal. How could I support anyone else? It would be a crime.

Simon Thomas, Gloucester

Welcome

My father would turn in his grave if he thought I even considered supporting anyone else. The passion, the spirit and fervour of the Swansea North Bank is unequalled, ask any of the opposition. West Ham were roared back all along the M4 after we knocked them out of the FA Cup in 1999, and many other so-called fashionable sides have had the same treatment – long may it last.

Martin Collip, Port Talbot

Cheers dad!

I first went to Swansea in 1957. Originally, I was from Ferndale in the Rhondda. I had been demobbed from the RAF and was shopping with my mother and father in the town. My father and I went to the

OFFICIAL PROGRAMME

3d.

SWANSEA
TOWN A.F.C.

LTD

SATURDAY, OCTOBER 9th, 1954

SWANSEA T. v. MIDDLESBRO

ENGLISH LEAGUE DIVISION II.   Kick Off 3.15 p.m.

Brian Nugent's first game watching Swansea.

85

Vetch Field and I have been hooked ever since.

Glanville Anstey, Bristol

A family thing

My family have always followed Swansea, ever since I can remember. My memories of early days are of Parkas, silk scarves, rattles, pitch invasions and generally dire football. This was the seventies, and it was incredible that the club climbed as high as they did and beat the best that the football world could put us up against.

Adrian Price, Banbury (ex-Brecon)

What an atmosphere

I remember well the railway sleepers on the East Terrace, and when I think of my early days at the Vetch I recall posters advertising the next four home matches. As if we wouldn't have gone! In the seventies it was all skinheads, black and white woollen scarves and a smell of reality in the air – as a kid that stays with you.

Nigel Drean, Newport

My home 'debut'

My first game was at The Vetch Field. We played Newcastle in the FA Cup third round. It was January 1965, and we won the game 1-0. I used to sneak in for free having pestered Herbie Williams for his autograph. There seemed to be regular defeats in those days though. They stand

out the most, but you can't change your team can you?

Phil Smith, Hereford

Seeing the light

Strange as it may seem, my first experiences of football were going to Ninian Park. I wanted to be different from the rest, so I followed Swansea Town. I caught the train from Bridgend to Swansea, having saved my pocket money up all month. Many Swans fans used to travel by train then from the South Glamorgan area, especially Bridgend. My first game was against Middlesbrough on Saturday 9th October 1954. We were in Division Two at the time and we won 2-0 with goals from Terry Medwin and Ivor Allchurch (who else). It was not uncommon to travel back on the train at 5.30 p.m. to Bridgend and see a lot of the visiting team on there too. A fantastic day for me was when I was a 'director for the day' and spent the day behind the scenes at the club and travelling to Barnet. We won 1-0 too, which made for a memorable day out. I shall never forget that day – to Pat, David and Martin all I can say is a very big 'thank you' for a wonderful birthday present. I have found that football gives immense pleasure to many people, no matter the topic the talk can go on for hours.

Brian Nugent, Leominster

Cover up

My mates all followed Cardiff City as I hail from the northern valleys of South Wales. I have always felt like a football alien, as

Brian Nugent rubs shoulders with the Swansea elite.

I now live in Rhyl which is a Wrexham stronghold. Having said that, it's better than living in Cardiff as I did. I used to go to Ninian with my mates and have to bite my lip when Swansea were there. As usual we won a lot at Ninian, and at times I got carried away and shouted with joy when the Swans scored. It soon had to be followed by a dose of acting to cover up the joy – some obscenities or something – or I would have been lynched.

Gareth Jones, Rhuddlan, North Wales

Away from home

My first away trip to see the Swans was in 1990 when we lost to Stoke City at their place. My mates Gary, Nozza and Lee were there too, they went with the supporters club. I remember laughing so much when Lee got ejected for blowing up a condom. Going away from home is so different to home games, you tend to get more passionate about it – home games are not the same.

Simon Roberts, Weston-super-Mare
(ex-Neath)

The first taste

My first game is as fresh in the memory now as it has ever been – Thursday 21st February 1946 at home to Derby County. I was once referred to in a book by David Farmer as I was one of the Dynevor schoolboys. Standing in such a huge crowd at the top of the North Bank stirred me, and that feeling has never left me to this day. Reg Weston and Jim Feeney were my favourite all-time players, but you couldn't get much better than the James boys (Leighton and Robbie) and Alan Curtis. Roger Freestone too is a joy to watch; tremendous players on their day. Every Swansea success is a joy to me. I hail from Townhill, and although I live away now the club is very close to my heart.

Stan Richards, Shropshire

Thanks John

I have been going to the Vetch since I was about ten years of age, they are my hometown team. My most treasured memory is that of Tosh climbing above everyone to head us to victory and ultimately to promotion from Division Three in 1979. What a story went on from there!

Ron Richards, Bristol

All right mate?

The club, as a rule, are friendly. I went to Ireland for a pre-season tour in 1999, and we travelled with the team to a number of games. They were very friendly and seemed to be glad to see us all there. That's the difference between a club like Swansea and,

Gareth Jones, a legal alien.

ON THE BALL . . .

For full coverage of Swansea City F.C. and the soccer scene, together with all the results, tables, news and views of the sporting scene . . .

ORDER YOUR COPY OF THE

SPORTING POST

STILL ONLY 10p

**Every Saturday!
Order your copy from
your local Newsagent now**

On the ball City … a clip from the local paper in 1999.

Gary and friends with ex-Chairman Steve Hamer.

say, a Premiership club. Even if we did get back there it would still be the same – still friendly but bigger!

Gary Martin, Llanelli

A team for life

I have been going to see the Swans since 1953. First of all it was on Saturday mornings to see Swansea schoolboys play. My father used to sing the praises of a young Scottish lad who was at Huddersfield at the time. He took me to see him play at the Vetch in 1956. His name was Dennis Law and, yes, he was a great player. I saw Swansea line-ups featuring both Allchurch brothers, Terry Medwin and Harry Griffiths. My

favourite tale goes back to 1934. My father and grandfather went from our hometown of Whitland to see Swansea Town play. It was in the FA Cup third round against Stoke City. Stoke had another legend playing for them at the time, Stanley Matthews. The away team were leading at half-time 1-0 through Matthews, who was never a noted goal-getter. He scored with his head that day, which was even more remarkable. During the half-time break a black cat ran across the front of the West Terrace and, yes you guessed it, the Swans scored four goals in the second half without reply. During the 1959/60 season I used to get down to the Vetch and watch the North Bank roof being constructed. I was at Dynevor at the time. The next season the floodlights went up, and the official opening was against Hibernian – the final score was 4-4. Most of the crowd had never seen a live floodlit match before and it was packed. The gasps around the ground when the lights were switched on were of disbelief. It was like a summer's day. I also saw Matthews at the Vetch in the sixties – he gave Harry Griffiths the run-around that day, Stoke winning 1-0. My most treasured memory was when we played Manchester United in a friendly just after the Munich air disaster. Matt Busby led a very good side out, Bobby Charlton and all. The 20,000 crowd applauded them for at least five minutes. I've loved every minute of being a Swans fan, and hope to love many more. The memories are treasured ones, and I could not imagine what things would have been like without the Swans at my side throughout my life.

Ron Griffiths, Hemel Hempstead

Quick March

I will never forget the parade through the city when the Swans were promoted to Division One – packed streets and a real party atmosphere. This was the reason I had followed them through thick and thin since 1959 when Len Allchurch and Mel Charles graced our club colours. The ups and downs of FA Cup glory, Welsh Cup finals, European adventures and even re-election were all fresh in the memory, but we had

The players relax on the 1999 tour of Eire. From left to right: Martin Thomas, Jon Coates, Jason Smith.

The great Swans side of 1958/59. The famous line-up includes Len Allchurch, Mel Charles, Harry Griffiths and goalkeeper.

Emyr Williams remembers the happy days of promotion as well as the not-so heady days of relegation.

Darren Bradley with his best mate, John Smith!

done it and I was very proud to be a Swan.

Emyr Williams, Pontardawe, Swansea

More than just a game

It's not just about the football, I love travelling with my mates as much as the ninety minutes. I would never have had half as good a time if it wasn't for the group of fans I travel with. Those are the best memories, the stop offs, the journeys and the laughs. You can't beat that. There is nothing better than travelling with like-minded people to games – genuine fans, that's football.

Darren Bradley, Gloucester

Authors' note

We hope you enjoyed this insight into what attracts people to the Vetch. For successful, winning football, and treasured losses! In many cases it's as a result of pride in the city itself. Swansea City supporters come from all walks of life and are found all over the world. Contrary to popular opinion, they are a friendly bunch of people who care very much for their football club and their country. Remember, supporters of Swansea City have seen the very best beaten by their team and also seen them lose to the very worst – how many other clubs can boast that kind of record? Being a Swansea City supporter is a roller-coaster ride in itself

Keith and Andy of the Gloucester Jacks warm up for some football with a few beers.

and you should remember that fans of other outwardly more successful teams are secretly envious of what we have to put up with!

Keith Haynes and Phil Sumbler

CHAPTER 7

From the Vetch to Wembley

Every football supporter's dream is to see their team at Wembley. For some supporters it's an almost annual pilgrimage up Wembley Way and to the twin towers. As a young Swansea fan, I used to watch the Cup Final every year on television and dream that one day I would see Swansea City climb the famous steps and lift a trophy. Swansea City attended Wembley twice, once leaving victorious and once beaten. Eighty-two years into their history, Swansea City made their debut at Wembley stadium in the Autoglass Trophy final of 1994. The game itself finished 1-1 after Swansea had led as early as the seventh minute. In the penalty shoot-out, it was Swansea that became victorious by converting four penalties to two. Three years and one month after the Autoglass victory, Swansea City headed back up Wembley Way for the Division Three play-off final against Northampton Town. The match was heading into injury time when the referee awarded Northampton a free kick, which (at the second attempt) was converted by John Frain to condemn Swansea to another season in the basement division. The kick that hit the back of the net was the last kick of the match. In this chapter, we look at memories of Swansea in the 'old' stadium and, as you can imagine, this focuses on good and bad stories of two very memorable days.

Can't face the pain

I remember when the game finished at Wembley and penalties loomed. The chap next to me stood up and left, as he couldn't bear the pressure of penalties. I remember thinking of him when we celebrated winning the trophy. I wonder if he regrets leaving then?

Phil Sumbler, Clydach, Swansea

Hungry sir?

I have never seen such an intense game. As the penalties were being taken, I couldn't help but chew the top of my flagpole. It must have got to me, because after we won I went to wave the flag in celebration and it fell down the stick!

Dai Davies, Port Tennant, Swansea

Line 'em up

I started drinking very early that morning and by the time the match started I was in

The programme for the 1994 Autoglass final against Huddersfield Town.

such a state that I don't remember much about it all. The one thing that I remember is that we outsung the Huddersfield fans despite there being twice as many of them. Mind you this could be the alcohol influence!

Nick Rees, Russia

A brave man

There are not many things that make me cry, but watching the team I had supported for so long take the field at Wembley, I shed many tears.

Shane Sinclair, Plasmarl, Swansea

Crystal ball

There are two things about the Autoglass final that really stick out in my mind. The first is singing the Welsh National Anthem at the 'home of football'. That part was an experience not to be forgotten, and one I would recommend to every Welshman. The other part was that sitting next to me in the stand was Jimmy Hadziabdic's son – he must have had third sight as he successfully predicted the outcome of every penalty!

Chris Wathan, Cardiff

Spare towel?

After the game had finished we headed into Wandsworth to continue the celebrations. We managed to find a house with a party going on and decided that we should gatecrash it. When we finally

got in we filled the bath to the top with beer. Watching several Swansea supporters swimming in this bath was a sight for sore eyes!

Mike Davies, London

OP's

Tobacco manufacturers must have had a field day that day at Wembley as I even took up smoking because the game was so tense. I had gone to Wembley with three of my friends on the train from Swansea and we stood there and prayed for victory when the penalties were being taken.

Mark Goddard, Llanelli

Seeing is believing

What I couldn't believe was that although there were supposed to be twice as many Huddersfield fans, every pub you passed on the North Circular had Swansea fans overflowing outside and there wasn't a Huddersfield fan in sight. After the penalties when Swansea collected the trophy, all I could see was the tip when every player lifted it up for the fans to see.

Mark Samuel, Morriston, Swansea

Bird's eye view

At Wembley, I was the closest supporter to the presentation party and could almost touch the Autoglass Trophy. I did get to touch it at a later date in the Harry

Griffiths bar and felt so proud as I lifted it up!

Daniel Merchant, Dunvant, Swansea

Got your skates on?

I didn't manage to get to Wembley that day because I was on a youth club outing in, of all places, Cardiff. We had been ice-skating all day and after boarding the bus to head back to Swansea, I tuned in my radio to find that the match had gone into extra time. I kept the bus updated throughout the rest of the game, including the penalties and, after Freestone saved the winning penalty, the whole bus erupted with celebration. I can imagine what those at Wembley felt like.

Chris Stevens, Dunvant, Swansea

Long arm of the Laur'

When the players were on a lap of honour of Wembley with the trophy, I managed to get a sneak touch on it through the fence.

Laura Croft, Neath

The Jack Highway

I was up with the lark that day. We travelled up the M4 – or the 'Jack Highway' as it was known for one day only as cars and buses were full of Swansea fans and festooned with flags, banners, scarves and posters. We even saw one funeral limousine complete with flags out of the

windows, presumably not on the way to a funeral.

John Hughes, Tenby

Super Mac

I sat in the Olympic Gallery at Wembley for the Autoglass final and can still hardly believe that Andy Macfarlane scored our goal in that game. I remember also thinking when the Huddersfield player ran in to take the kick that he was taking it too quickly and he was going to miss – and he did!

Liam James

Appropriation

I remember pulling into a service station in the bus on the way home. A mini-bus pulled in beside us and out poured about fifteen fans who then proceeded to pull out the 'Autoglass Winners' sign that had been on the Wembley pitch! God knows how they managed to get it off the pitch in the first place and then out of the stadium afterwards – even now I still imagine these people carrying the sign down the steps from Wembley.

Phil Sumbler, Clydach, Swansea

Oh the pain…

I couldn't afford the travel back to London for the game and had to stay at home in Bermuda. If you guys thought that the penalties were nerve-wracking then you should have seen me for the two days that

I had to wait for the result. I never want to experience a feeling like that again.

Mark James, Southampton, Bermuda

Butty brigade

My family's coach arrived at a pub in London and was told 'You're the Mountain Dew and your sandwiches are in the back' – we were surprised but we ate them. Half an hour later the MD bus turned up and the landlady's face was a picture when she'd realized what had happened.

Gary Elsey, Gorseinon, Swansea

Everywhere we go

We played Huddersfield on my thirty-seventh birthday. I was in tears at the final whistle and turned and hugged my brother Clive and my mate Johnnie Aspell. After the game, as we travelled back up the M6 to Macclesfield, we passed loads of Swansea fans – it was as if they were everywhere that day.

Paul Barrett, West Cross, Swansea

(Swansea City 0-1 Northampton Town Third Division play-off final – Saturday 24 May 1997)

Gutted 1

When we played Northampton, it was a horrible day for me as my mum had died the day before. The fact that we lost the game

so cruelly just about summed up that period of my life in a nutshell.

Jez Welch, Preston

Gutted 2

When the free-kick was awarded, I knew that they were going to score. When the original kick was blocked I thought that was it but to see a re-take and the goal coming from that was too much. I left the ground in total despair and promptly bumped into my cousin who was a policeman on duty in London for the day – that cheered me up a bit.

Andy Fuge, Nottingham

True 1

At the time nothing would have cheered me up, but the fact that two years later Northampton were relegated did, as I knew they weren't good enough to last in the higher division. Sadly, I don't think we would have lasted too long either.

Matthew Parsell, Aberdare

True 2

I travelled to Wembley that day with my son. We were ticketless, but just had to be at the ground even if it were just to soak up the atmosphere. I made and held up a huge placard asking if anyone had any spare tickets. After a while, some kind soul sold me two tickets at the face value of £28 each. Apparently (so he said)

"THE ONLY WAY IS UP"
97
PLAY OFFS
Nationwide

Nationwide
FOOTBALL LEAGUE
3

Division 3
Play-Off Final

Northampton Town
v
Swansea City

Saturday 24th May 1997

Kick Off 3.00pm
Official Matchday Programme £3.50

The programme for the 1997 Division Three play-off final against Northampton.

these were from Doug Sharpe's personal allocation.

Adrian O'Connor, Middlesex

Examination

The worst part about the defeat was that the next day I had to go into school and start my GCSEs. It wasn't the way to relax in preparation for them.

Laura Croft, Neath

Gutted 3

We were all over Northampton that day and clearly (from my biased point of view) deserved to win the game. Carl Heggs was playing the game of his life and if it wasn't for the idiot referee we would have won the game and promotion.

Tim Jones, Dunvant, Swansea

Bizarre 1

This was the single most bizarre day of my life. The Swansea fans, despite being outnumbered two to one, sang with a passion that created an atmosphere like no other. Northampton's goal was against the run of play from a re-taken free-kick in injury time. Grown men all around me burst into tears – I don't know if I will ever experience such a day of mixed emotions again!

Chris Stevens, Dunvant, Swansea

Armchair agony

I watched the Northampton game from my home on Sky Television (I was living in Scotland at the time). I remember feeling as gutted as any Swans supporter that was there on the day.

Kevin McCarry, London

Bizarre 2

The game itself was pathetic, with neither side seemingly capable of any decent football. Having said that, Northampton deserved to win less than we did and for them to score in the ninetieth minute was a travesty.

Chris Ollier, Dunvant, Swansea

Gutted

As we walked out of the ground that day at Wembley, I jumped straight into a black cab to head back to work with my mate in Camden Town (a slightly extended lunchbreak!). I can remember holding my head in my hands for the whole journey back and refused to work when we eventually got there. After a while I decided that I should persuade everyone to come down the pub with me to drown my sorrows, which they all did – a good example to set seeing as I was the boss.

Mike Davies, Crouch End, London

A Swans fan sums up the feeling of losing at Wembley.

Gutted 5

All our hopes and aspirations for the season were crushed by one cruel refereeing decision. I remember feeling it was like watching in slow motion as the free-kick sailed into the corner of the net. That is the closest I have ever been to crying at a football match. I hope I never have to experience a feeling like that again.

Phil Sumbler, Clydach, Swansea

Bizarre 3

All I remember is an unreal feeling as I saw the ball hit the back of the net. There was a delay of a second or two then all the Northampton fans rose as one, with a massive roar following soon after. The silence was deadly our end of the ground.

Mark Goddard, Llanelli

Swans fans 1 Cobblers fans 0

I was depressed at the start of the game because we had only taken 16,000 supporters with us compared to Northampton's 25,000. Having said that, from where we were sat we completely out-sang them on the day. I was stunned into silence for ages after Northampton had scored.

Paul Barrett, West Cross, Swansea

Gutted 6

I was ready for the game to head into extra-time, as was everybody who stood around me. When John Frain took the free-kick it was clear that Roger was not going to get to the ball and as it hit the back of the net, all I felt was my heart being ripped from my body.

Daniel Jones, Pontardawe, Swansea

Not my favourite year

After the game, I sat in my armchair at home and refused to talk to anyone and even refused to go to the pub with my friends. I was like a child who didn't get his own way – although I was thirty-two at the time.

Huw Mellor, Marcham, Oxon

What comes around

The worst part was walking back down Wembley Way after the game and seeing the smug looks on the Northampton fans' faces – you would have thought they'd show some compassion. I'd have loved to have been there when they lost their play-off final the next year just to get my own back on them.

Ian Wishart, Swansea

Don't give up the day job

I was commentating on the game for the hospital radio at Morriston Hospital. When the ball hit the back of the net at Wembley, there was complete silence on air for about a minute as I was too gutted to speak and had no idea how I was going to explain it to sick people!

Shane Sinclair, Plasmarl, Swansea

Sweetners

This was almost a great day. I had a sixteen-hour flight into Heathrow and stayed at the Wembley Hilton. Drank with the Northampton manager and had a good few beers with Wyndham Evans, Jeremy Charles and a few others. Before the game, I spoke to Arsene Wenger and John Hartson and walked down Wembley Way with John Cornforth. 'Super John' was mobbed by Swans fans singing 'Swansea till you die' which is a proud moment that I will always remember. As for the game? – ah, that was a fix!

Nick Rees, Russia

No compassion

I didn't realise it was possible for Wembley to be so cold. People had arrived in T-shirts and left in jumpers and coats. To make it worse we lost – I don't expect I would have noticed the cold had we won promotion that day!

Gary Martin, Llanelli

Gutted 7

It hurt so much that day to see the Northampton fans celebrating in the way

Lee Haynes in a happier moment before the trip to Wembley.

that we had only three years before – I knew then how the Huddersfield fans must have felt that April afternoon in 1994. The other thing that sticks out in my mind that day was that Jan Molby did not play well at all, which was one huge disappointment.

Dai Davies, Port Tennant, Swansea

An early lesson

We should have beaten Northampton: they were not very good, we had Jan Molby and the referee I think was not at all good. I wasn't happy on my way home and didn't feel very well for a long time after it.

Lee Haynes, Northampton

Authors' note

As you have seen from these two accounts, watching your team at Wembley (or even listening or watching elsewhere) can make you experience emotions that you have not felt before. Watching us lift the Autoglass Trophy in 1994 was one of my highs in watching Swansea, and likewise the defeat by Northampton was a low that I hope I don't experience too often. There is no doubt that Wembley is every supporter's dream – I just hope that if or when we get there (or at least to the new stadium) again it is a celebration on the way home. To me, losing at Wembley was summed up by a notice in a car on the trip back from the Northampton game – it said 'Swansea 0 Northampton 1 – We wuz robbed!'

Keith Haynes and Phil Sumbler

CHAPTER 8

Moments to forget

Swansea fans have had more then their fair share of both good and bad memories. The club was wound up in December 1985 before being saved from extinction and, of course, we were relegated all the way down the divisions as quickly as we went up them. We have known the agony of losing in play-off finals and FA Cup semi-finals. In this chapter we will look at moments that most Swansea supporters would rather forget.

Just a little more time

It was a sad day for Swansea City when Jan Molby was sacked as manager. He was a good personality, but the club did not see eye to eye with the Great Dane. If he had been given a chance he would have led us to promotion that season.

Christopher Ormesher

Corker – not!

The season under Alan Cork was a complete disaster. After the agony of Wembley the previous season, there was nothing to

be positive about as the team stumbled from one nightmare to another. This was definitely the lowest that I have ever seen the club.

Chris Ollier, Dunvant, Swansea

Innocents abroad

There was one game at Portsmouth and we stood on their end to watch the game. We were a group of young teens and were no angels, but we were no match for the Pompey fans who were big, old and all wore sheepskin coats!

Mike Morris, Ontario, Canada

Not my favourite game

When we played Fulham in the FA Cup first round, we lost the game at Craven Cottage 7-0. I went to the match with my best man and his girlfriend (her first-ever game) and just jumped up and cheered every time that Fulham scored, despite us being in the Swansea end. At the end of the match, I was so disgusted that I threw my scarf onto the pitch and immediately regretted it as I knew that I'd have to buy myself a new one.

Huw Mellor, Marcham

Reality

I always remember the relegation from the First Division and the harsh realisation setting in that we had bought our way to the top and could not sustain the cost of staying there. Sadly, support for this club never has been, and never will be, big enough to stay in the top flight of English football.

Stephen Richardson, Brentwood, Essex

Free fall

The downward spiral from the First Division to the Fourth Division were terrible years. Three relegations, the sacking of John Toshack and the eventual receivership were dark, dark days for Swansea City.

Mark Samuel, Morriston, Swansea

Crocodile tears

The day that it was announced that Swansea City were no more, I was Christmas shopping in Blackpool. In Boots they had *Grandstand* on the television and they were showing the demise of Swansea. I was only twelve at the time and stood there crying my eyes out.

Jez Welch, Preston

The only way is up

Watching Swansea lose 7-0 at Fulham in the FA Cup, I felt that the club had reached absolute rock bottom. This was a Second Division team losing to a Third Division team in such a poor manner – and it was freezing cold.

Gary Elsey, Gorseinon, Swansea

Don't do this at home

When we played Nuneaton Borough in the FA Cup, I stood on the North Bank in the pouring rain shouting total obscenities at the team. What I had forgotten was that I had my eleven-year-old niece with me for her first ever game – Whoops!

Andy Williams, Porthcawl

The silent majority

I don't get too worked up by the problems when we aren't playing that well because I remember all too well that terrible day when the club folded in December 1985. At that time, it was difficult to imagine life without Swansea City, and the way that I view things now is that it is better to have a poor club then no club at all.

Andy Fuge, Nottingham

Life and death

The tragic loss of Robbie James was a very low point, just eclipsed by the day that the 'closed' sign was put on the Vetch.

The thought of no more Swansea City is almost unthinkable and we came so close to this becoming reality. I was just so happy that the survival package was put together and that I am still able to talk about the club.

Mark James, Southampton, Bermuda

Same old story

When we played Leeds at home in 1982, I was frog-marched through the streets by my father just minutes before a running battle took place between rival sets of 'fans'.

Chris Stevens, Dunvant, Swansea

Never go back

When we re-appointed Terry Yorath as manager, the first game back was Bristol City at the Vetch. We lost the game 6-1 and I can remember all the Bristol City fans singing at us 'Yorath's back!' – my response was to wish that the bloke had never returned. Maybe there is something in the saying that you should never go back.

Phil Sumbler, Clydach, Swansea

Fatal error

Kevin Cullis was appointed as manager just before Molby took over and lasted just under a week and two matches. This was a complete fiasco and made Swansea a laughing stock. We had been promised

a 'big name' manager and were given this bloke that no-one had ever heard of.

Ian Jones, Cardiff

Just the job

When we went 2-0 up in the play-off semi against West Brom, I was watching the game with my mates Chris Rees, a Jack, and Chris Job, a West Brom fan. When the second went in there was absolute mayhem on the North Bank and Chris Job fell over as Chris Rees and myself went absolutely mental in the celebrations. We both thought that this was it and we were in Division One – sadly, history will show that we didn't.

Mark Goddard, Llanelli

I gave them everything

The day that the Swans went 'bust' I had been to the Caswell Bay hotel in the evening. I hadn't heard the news and when I came out of there (a little the worse for wear because of drink) my father told me that the Swans were bankrupt and had been closed down. I cried all the way home that night and passed all my savings on to try and save the club – all £52 of them!

Nick Rees, Russia

Wall written on

There was one game in a season that we were relegated. It was an away game at Meadow Lane against Notts County and it was the worst 0-0 game that I have ever seen. The writing was on the wall from that day forwards.

Adrian O'Connor, Ruislip, Middlesex

Wrong decade

The worst moment for me was when John Toshack left the club. This was the man that had built us into one of the forces at the time in English football and he was leaving us. He had also managed to bring the city together and made everybody proud of our football club. I still think that if he had done the same thing but ten years later, finances wouldn't have been a problem and we might still be there.

Stephen Godrich, Stevenage

And still?

We played Peterborough a few years back in the FA Cup and lost 3 or 4-1 on the night. That was bad enough, because we were complete rubbish at the time and demonstrated this to the watching nation. People on the North Bank argued amongst themselves between Jan Molby and Alan Cork and to cap it all I got beaten up in Castle Square.

Chris Wathan, Cardiff

Yesterday's news

I found out that the club had folded when I was stood on a platform at Bristol Temple Meads railway station. I can remember

seeing the back page of one of the newspapers which gave the headline that we had gone under and just choked up. Surely there couldn't be a life without a Swansea City Football Club?

Paul Barrett, West Cross, Swansea

Prophet John

The 7-0 defeat at Fulham a few years back was a terrible performance from the Swans. There was absolutely no effort or pride on the pitch from the players and, to me, this was rock bottom. I knew that the way we were playing there was no way that we were going to avoid relegation and, sadly, I was proved right.

John Williams, London

Down and down

The relegations back from the First to the Fourth Division happened so quickly that it seemed to wipe out the promotions that had taken place in the same time.

Andrew Fenton, Ontario, Canada

Do the 92

I went to one game at Peterborough on our way up to the First Division, which we lost 2-0. At that time, I was around fifteen short of the full ninety-two League grounds and, although I had been to Peterborough before, it was when they were a non-League club so I didn't think that it counted. I remember travelling back from that game thinking

Tosh is gone, an absolute nightmare for Swans fans. The inevitable decline had started.

'What a load of rubbish' and whether it was all worth it – the big ninety-two that is!

Vic Feldeth, Dunvant, Swansea

The worst of times

Being told that the Swans had folded at Christmas in 1985, I was so gutted I didn't speak to anyone for days – and then realized we'd been saved! I have to say Doug Sharpe did far more than anyone else did at the time. And to be honest, I know he left under a cloud, nobody, and I mean nobody has done anything quite like it since. He wore his heart on his sleeve, and saved the club, and even purchased players like Gilligan, Connor and Walker for serious money, again which has never been equalled. I just wish there were more chairman like him about. He was a Swans fan, and a good businessman, and he backed up his talk most of the time, unlike many other football chairman.

Keith Haynes, Gloucester

Inevitable conclusion

For me, there are two moments that really stick out in my mind as moments that I would rather forget. The first was the resignation of Frank Burrows – this was a man who had a proven track record at this level and we had let him go. He proved, in taking Cardiff out of Division Three, that he is a good manager. The other was the sacking of another manager, Jan Molby. The appointment of Molby in the first place had shown a high level of ambition within the club because he was a high-profile person

who had great connections within the game. He was extremely popular within the club and everybody felt a tinge of sadness when he left.

Matthew Parsell, Aberdare

CHAPTER 8

Views of Vetch Field

No matter whom you support, there is always one point in the ground that you prefer to watch matches from. It may be superstition, it may be the people that stand or sit near you or it may be because you don't know any different, but there is a favourite point for everyone. Hear we listen to Swansea supporters telling us where they watch the Swans from and why.

THE NORTH BANK

Milk crate fate

It seems strange to say that I used to sit on the North Bank, but I did in the lowest crowd for a League match (around 1,200) and someone behind me asked that day if I could sit down as I was on a milk crate at the time – sad times. I did have a season ticket in the stand for many years, but gave it up when Malcolm Struel asked for an extra £100 for its renewal – it was back to the North Bank for me then.

Vic Feldeth, Dunvant, Swansea

A real fix

It still sends a tingle down my spine when I walk up the steps on the right of the North Bank and get the first glimpse of the day of the hallowed Vetch Field turf.

Andy Williams, Porthcawl

Same old place

For the last twenty years at the Vetch, I have stood under the television gantry on the North Bank with some mates. I say mates, but really they are just faces that always stand in the same place as me. When I first went to the Vetch, I always used to stand on a ledge at the back of the North Bank. I only moved from there because I realized that I couldn't see all the action after a few years!

Paul Barrett, West Cross, Swansea

An aerial view of the Vetch Field from 1981.

It's all relative

The North Bank is a great place to stand because, as time goes on, you get to know all the people around you and their feelings towards certain players. It's like having a second family as you share jokes with them and your observations of the game. I don't get back as often as I'd like now I live away, but the last time I was there, the 'family' was asking where I'd been and how I was, etc.

Keiron McDonnell, Peterborough

Simply the best

I have tried watching a game at the Vetch from every possible viewpoint. Nothing though compares to the North Bank, which can get very emotional, joyous, annoyed, frustrated all at once. I don't think there is a ground in Britain that can rival it for atmosphere.

Mark James, Southampton, Bermuda

A view of the North Bank from the Centre Stand in April 2000.

A modern day view of the Swansea North Bank from the West Terrace.

Every avenue

I have stood and sat virtually everywhere at the Vetch; now I have a young son, I mainly watch from the East Stand even though it doesn't compare to the North Bank. I was so proud that my son, Adam, was able to sample the North Bank atmosphere for the FA Cup win over West Ham. Sadly, in the days of all-seater stadia these days will soon disappear.

John Hughes, Tenby

My spot

I always stand in the same position on the North Bank and always with the same people all around me. I tried to think why I always stand there and I guess that it's because that's where my father used to stand. I suppose you could call it a family tradition.

Mike Davies, Crouch End, London

Unrivalled

The thing that I love about standing on the North Bank is that the game can be played in sub-zero conditions and it's always warm there. The atmosphere generated from this terrace is second to none.

Gary Martin, Llanelli

THE WEST STAND (DOUBLE DECKER)

The West stand was demolished in the late 1980s after it was deemed unsafe. Many Swansea supporters will remember this stand and watching games from there

Oi – sit down

I used to love sitting in the West Stand when I was younger. The last time I went in there I must have been around ten or eleven, against Tottenham. Alan Curtis scored a pearler of a goal into the net in front of the stand and I missed it as everybody in there used to stand up when the action was that end of the pitch. Being only a nipper, when they stood up I couldn't see a thing...still enjoyed the goal mind!

Phil Sumbler, Clydach, Swansea

Thunder rising

The West Stand had the best view ever across the Vetch Field. I used to sit in there with my father and there were a great bunch of season ticket holders that used to sit all round us. I remember that the stand had a wooden floor, which I swear was for banging your feet on to create the famous 'West Stand Rumble'.

Andy Fuge, Nottingham

Come and join the DD's

The West Bank had a great view, and often there was a sizeable away support below us. You could see the North Bank and it swayed from side to side with over 15,000 fans in it. Then the old East Terrace opposite, a giant concrete terrace. I love the old double-decker West Bank, it was a shame it had to go.

Simon Thomas, Gloucester

Two shots from the camera of Nick Rees, taken from the Old Double Decker stand. To the right features Swansea versus Southampton and below is Swansea versus Liverpool. Both matches finished as victories for the home side. In the distance is the East Stand.

Family stand

My family are all season ticket holders for the Centre Stand and sit in the front with no obstructions at all in our view. I love the fact that most of the people around you are also season ticket holders and by the end of a season they are like family to you.

Laura Croft, Neath

Pint please, barman

I always prefer sitting in the Centre Stand because at half-time you can disappear into the Harry Griffiths bar instead of queuing in the wind and rain for pasties.

Daniel Merchant, Dunvant, Swansea

Do the Ayatollah!

Like the dandruff of a Chernobyl handgrenade tester – there is a Centre Stand ritual that is so unique that its perfect synchronization makes the Red Army look like a hyperactives' convention. It goes something like this: Matthew Bound clears the ball onto the Centre Stand roof. There follows five dull thuds as the ball bounces its way down the apex. Shaken from the rafters, a toxic mixture of asbestos and rust descends gently on the heads of spectators who then,

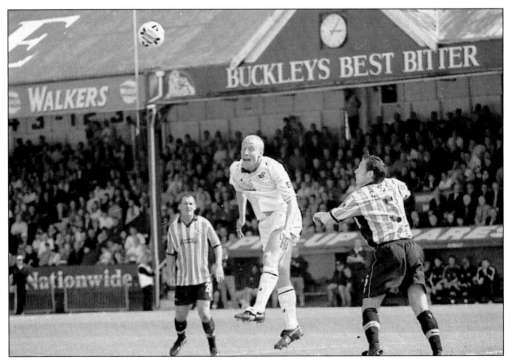

A view of the old Buckley's clock above the Centre Stand. Housed below this are the home and away dug-outs, and behind them the various board members from both clubs of the day.

in unison, splutter and pat their barnets in a vain attempt to remove the embedded flakelets.

Anthony Thomas, Margam

THE EAST STAND

Bring your brolly

I have watched games from both the North Bank and the East Stand and, unlike a lot of people, I prefer the East Stand. The view of the game from there is incredible and completely unobstructed. Mind you, it gets a little wet when it starts raining.

Chris Stevens, Dunvant, Swansea

Eagle eyed

I wouldn't say the East Stand was my favourite position because it used to be the old West Stand, but since that was deemed unfit, the East Stand has been the nearest I can get to that view. I do believe that sometimes the manager should watch the game from there as you can see absolutely everything that is going on.

Stephen Richardson, Brentwood, Essex

Hello, hello, hello

The East Stand has the best view in the Football League, no doubt about it, and you can see the formations of the teams so clearly. Also there are some real characters in there. One chap called 'Les' regularly

shouts the most obscure things and there is sometimes a chap with a trumpet – he's awful, the police took it away from him once because he put off a Cardiff player taking a free kick.

Lee Sanders, Haverfordwest

Stranger and stranger

I used to take my trumpet into the games and sit in the East Stand, but the club told me not to because I was putting off the opposition at penalties and free-kicks. I leave it to 'Old Les' now to put them off with his high-pitched, very emotive comments. I am sure his voice is set at 'screech' on Saturdays only, any other times he sounds normal. His favourite shout for the Derby cup game was 'Ferrets, I like a lump of ferrets on my toast'. He shouted it at least ten times along with 'I've got feet' and 'There's a dog in my seat'. A very odd man indeed.

Tim Kemp, Swansea

Jester laugh

I have been in the East Stand since I was six…I just wish my dad would come and get me out, I've eaten loads of pasties, and seen all the games since 1980!

The Pie Boy, Llanelli

Leave my dad alone

My dad, a season-ticket holder since 1978, got out of his seat in the awful 1984/85 season and shouted 'That's it I've seen enough, I'm going home'. As he left we scored, he came back and said to me 'Those buggers just can't let a man have a peaceful life can they'. He has been a season ticket holder ever since.

Carl Morrison, Swansea

Mike's got the job

I remember when John Bond was the manager. He came into the bar in the East Stand and said to me 'What formation do you think we should we play today Mike?' I knew then that he was not long for the Vetch Field hot-seat.

Mike Cabriani, Swansea

As you can see, Swansea supporters have very differing reasons for viewing the game from where they stand or sit. Generally, those on the North Bank tend to be there for the atmosphere while those in the stands are there for a variety of reasons ranging from best views to being near a bar! These memories will last people a lifetime and in twenty-five years hence people will have different favourite viewpoints in the new stadium.

CHAPTER 10

Local Derbies

One of the things about football that make people love it so, is its derby games. Many people talk about the Glasgow derby and the Merseyside derby as big games that have no equal. For fans of Swansea City, there is no derby that matters other than the one against nearest rivals Cardiff City. This to many of them is more than a football match and, sadly, has seen outbreaks of serious violence in recent years. This has led to a stage where away fans were excluded from the derby games and, although they have now been allowed back in, supporters are escorted on buses all the way along the thirty-five-mile trip from ground to ground. This is something that does not happen in other derby games. Here, Swansea fans share some of their experiences of watching their team play against Cardiff City. The hooliganism that has become a part of this fixture is not to be celebrated in any way, but we have included some stories relating to violent incidents within this chapter because some of it does stand out in the minds of the supporters. But of course it was not always like this. There was a time in the early part of the 1920s and right up to the '60s that Cardiff and Swansea fans travelled to each other's big games because it was Wales who were being represented. This

cutting from the South Wales Daily Post in 1925 confirms this, and makes you think.

The cup final – 800 from Swansea

The Jubilee Cup final at Wembley on Saturday afternoon, the first being played in 1875, has an international aspect. For the first time in forty years two nations meet. Fifty years ago the FA Cup started, forty years ago Blackburn played Queens Park, an England - Scotland encounter. On Saturday it's Cardiff City of Wales against Sheffield United of England. Thousands of merry trippers make their way to Wembley and will be marshalled by 400 constables, 400 stewards and over 100 attendants. They will be joined by 100 ambulancemen. Throughout the night the association supporters made their way to Wembley and hawkers did a ready trade in the teams' colours. Coffee stalls were lunched at and sightseeing tours were a-plenty. The stadium formed a beautiful picture with its centre of brilliant emerald, so finely rolled and mowed it looked like a vicarage lawn. Many

The ugly face of the South Wales derby, which has tainted the fixture since the early seventies. These hateful scenes were seen in December 1993 at Ninian Park between so-called Swansea and Cardiff fans, when the game was held up for so long it seemed that it would never finish. Since then the games have either been played with away fans banned or with the help of a massive police operation to keep the fans apart.

enthusiastic Welshmen whiled away the time outside the gates by singing their native songs. Hilarity ceased at the Cenotaph and the football enthusiasts ranged themselves in reverent fashion. Impulsively they laid the area with button-holed flowers and bunches of flowers *in memoriam*. The people from all over Wales then made their way to Wembley, some 75,000 attending the Wembley final.

South Wales Daily Post, *1925*

Swansea to Wembley

Swansea devotees of the soccer code have been in a dilemma during the past week or so, shall we go to Plymouth or to Wembley? This was the question they repeatedly asked themselves. On Friday night 300 persons boarded the High Street train at 11 p.m. They were set for London, for Wembley and the cup final. Agog with excitement they were dressed in their splendid blue. A fair number joined them from Port Talbot, Neath and neighbouring towns. At the same time Swansea fans made their way by the hundred south to Plymouth for the town's crucial game down there. In all fifty-six trains went to London, all football specials run by GWR and heading to Paddington. The six-hour journey a pleasure. About twenty more trains went from Cardiff to London. Bigger crowds travelled by the LM and S railway fleet from Swansea to London.

Typical South Wales derby scenes – all in the name of football.

Two trains being run, one from Victoria and one from St Thomas. Another 500 made the journey by this route. It is expected that Cardiff and Swansea soccer fans will have much to cheer come the final whistles this weekend as both areas celebrate victories for Wales.

South Wales Daily Post, 1925

Changed times

Those days of shared excitement for the teams of Cardiff and Swansea are sadly over. In those days, devotees of the soccer code, as they were called, were as one. Nowadays you are either blue or you are white – there is no middle ground. I recall one Ron Jones, now a national radio commentator, doing the Swansea *v.* Cardiff Welsh Cup final in the early eighties. He shouted excitedly as Cardiff equalised. 'Cardiff have scored, we have scored' – of course the Swans went on to win 2-1...naturally!

Keith Haynes, Gloucester

1993

I was at the game that night and hated every minute of it, I was terrified. We spent most of the game waiting for a large skinhead standing in front of us to turn round to us and declare that he was a Cardiff fan. He didn't but he was wearing a large amount of Blue and White. I'm still not convinced he wasn't a Cardiff fan.

Andy Williams, Porthcawl

Goodwill to all men

It was four days before Christmas and we got into Ninian Park for free because the local constabulary feared a crush and opened the gate to let all the Swansea fans in. As we walked into the ground there were chairs flying through the air. The man standing next to me got hit by one in the head and fell down in a pool of blood. I didn't watch the game at all that night, I was just watching out for the chairs flying through the air.

Mark Goddard, Llanelli

Come in number two

Swansea fans will still taunt Cardiff fans with a rendition of 'Swim Away, Swim Away' – this relates to a story of football violence on Swansea Beach. There were about fifty of them in total and when the Swansea fans charged at them, they jumped into Swansea Bay and started swimming for it. It was comical stuff, in a way, that you don't see every day. However, these scenes have tainted the games for a long time and is very sad indeed. I just wish we could all go and watch the games together, but I suppose that will never happen.

Gary Elsey, Gorseinon, Swansea

Proof of the pudding

All Swansea fans will tell you that the local media is biased towards Cardiff City. Proof of this, for me, came on New Year's Day 1980 when Swansea beat Cardiff 2-1 at the Vetch. David Giles scored the winner in the ninetieth minute, just five minutes after Cardiff had hit the underside of the Swansea crossbar. I left the game and rushed home to watch the goals on the local news but BBC Wales did not show it. Now if that isn't bias…

Andy Fuge, Nottingham

The tension

Part of the thing that I like about derby games is not necessarily the performance or the result on the pitch. I always look out for the extra special atmosphere that is at both grounds as the away supporters turn up.

Mark James, Southampton, Bermuda

Seeing both sides

I have only ever been to one derby game and that was last season. I now live in Cardiff and it is frightening to see the hatred that some Cardiff fans have for Swansea fans.

Laura Croft, Neath

The real reason

Derby games against Cardiff are second to none. The atmosphere inside the ground is electric and you know that you can't afford to lose the game. I can remember winning 2-1 at Ninian Park one Easter Monday, which relegated Cardiff and effectively secured our

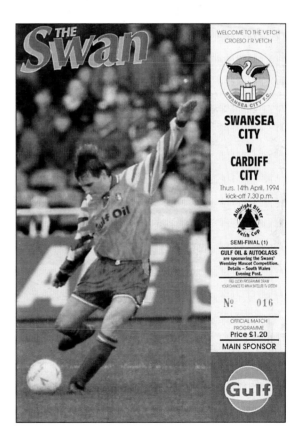

The Swan *programme for the Swansea versus Cardiff home clash in April 1994.*

own safety in the division. Moments like that are what football is all about.

Phil Sumbler, Clydach, Swansea

He'll never make it

I was in the East Stand one derby game with my father. Half time arrived and the Bluebirds were winning 2-0. My father's voice rung out loud in the stand with the words 'The first thing they should do is get that number seven off, he's useless'. That number seven was a certain Dean Saunders, he wasn't taken off and scored a second half hat-trick in a 3-2 win for the Swans. Nice one Dad!

Chris Stevens, Dunvant, Swansea

In-bred

Winning derby games was always important to me as it gave me the chance to crow over the Cardiff fans who think that they are Wales' premier club. Now I live and work in Cardiff, I get this feeling every time that they lose again, irrespective of who the opposition are.

Ian Jones, Cardiff

New ball please

We played Cardiff one year in the snow at the Vetch. The game started with an orange ball and Swansea were 4-0 up within the first half hour. They then switched back to the white ball and Swansea won the game 4-1. Maybe we should always play with an orange ball?

Daniel Merchant, Dunvant, Swansea

Proper abuse

Obviously part of a derby game is the banter that the supporters throw at the opposing fans and players. I can remember one game in the late 1970s where Cardiff had a player we referred to as 'Duck Foot Dwyer' playing for them. The Swansea fans spent most of the game shouting 'quack quack' at him.

Mike Davies, London

You are out

I can see it now, Jimmy Gilligan hammering home a goal against Cardiff City in the FA Cup at the Vetch Field. Sheer class was Jimmy, and how he celebrated that goal! We won 2-1 and the looks on the faces of those Cardiff City fans was priceless.

Daniel Webb, Swansea

Anté Cardiff

Swansea played Cardiff in the Welsh Cup final in 1983 and both sides were playing end-to-end stuff when one Cardiff forward broke clear of the Swansea defence and was bought down by Ante Rajkovic, resulting in his sending off. Far from blaming him, I just thought he was a hero for stopping the Cardiff player scoring what looked a certain goal. He still joined in the lap of honour after we had won the Welsh Cup in front of 22,000 Swansea fans – and the Cardiff fans thought that they were loud! Also there was a game before Alan Davies tragically took his own life, when we 2-0

The Bluebird *programme for the Swansea versus Cardiff away match in December 1993.*

down against Cardiff and came back to draw 2-2 – performances like that against Cardiff are to be treasured.

Nick Rees, Russia

Victory – again

The last time we played Cardiff at the Vetch, they arrived extremely cocky about getting the result against us. They went 1-0 up very early in the match and looked likely to get the result that they were expecting. They didn't reckon though with one of the best battling performances I have ever seen from a Swansea City team as they came back to win the game 2-1 with a goal in the last minute. That sent

them back to Cardiff happy!

Steven Godrich, Stevenage

The stuff that dreams are made of

The year that we played them in the snow and won 4-1, the crowd on the North Bank were united in their singing of 'I'm dreaming of a white Christmas'.

Dai Davies, Port Tenant, Swansea

Super Jim

We drew Cardiff in the FA Cup in 1991 and were 1-0 down when Cardiff missed an open goal. Jimmy Gilligan then scored a goal out of nowhere and stood in front of all the Cardiff supporters to celebrate. We went on to win the game and all the Cardiff fans ended the game crying…couldn't happen to nicer people.

John Williams, London

Even those in authority

The funniest thing that I have ever seen at a football match happened in a derby game. It was the Welsh Cup final of 1982 and Swansea were winning 2-1 in the 89th minute. Swansea were down to ten men and a Cardiff player went to retrieve the ball from in front of the North Bank to take a quick throw-in. Just as he was about to pick the ball up, a steward stepped in front of him and kicked the ball away – priceless!

Andy Fuge, Nottingham

It cannot happen here

There was one bizarre moment, almost surreal, when Cardiff were due to play Wrexham in the Welsh Cup final. The game was to be held at the Vetch and they opened the North Bank for any Swansea fans that wanted to watch the game. It was a weird feeling being in the Vetch where you normally stand, surrounded by Cardiff fans one side and Wrexham fans the other side. Cardiff went on to win the cup with a corking goal from Alan Curtis. It was painful to see their fans on 'our' pitch lifting Curtis and the Welsh Cup onto their shoulders.

Phil Sumbler, Clydach, Swansea

Elemental mascot jousting

I remember Cardiff coming down to the Vetch for a game in around 1968 which they won 3-1, with a nineteen-year-old John Toshack scoring two or three goals for Cardiff. Their element of idiots ran across the North Bank and there was mayhem everywhere in the ground. Another funny moment came around fifteen years ago when one of their fans thumped the Swansea mascot of the time. Although it was a Cardiff fan on the Swansea mascot it was quite bizarre to watch.

Paul Barrett, West Cross, Swansea

Some Swansea fans will class Barry Town as a local derby because it is only six miles outside of Cardiff. Although not the 'real' derby, here we see two stories of rival experiences involving Barry Town.

Dialect mistake

A few years ago, Barry drew Aberdeen in the third round of the UEFA cup. I lived in Aberdeen at the time and draped my flag which said 'Aberdeen Jacks' on it. The Barry fans starting taunting the flag with songs of 'You Jack b******'. Amusingly, the Aberdeen fans thought that they were singing Jock instead of Jack and responded accordingly with songs of my own. All that tension from just one flag.

Shane Sinclair, Swansea

Swansea mascot, Cyril the Swan.

Watch the game?

We played Barry one year in the Welsh Cup final. The first leg was scheduled for Ninian Park and there were about 200 or so Swansea fans there. The game wasn't up to much and the Swansea fans spent most of the second half doing a conga round the terrace singing 'We know a song that gets on everybody's nerves'. I'm not sure the Barry fans knew what to make of it.

Phil Sumbler, Clydach, Swansea

Whoever you support, there is nothing like a derby game to get the blood boiling and every supporter will tell you that this is the one game that they want to win above all others when the fixture lists are released every July. The Swansea and Cardiff derby is unique, in that no club has ever completed a League 'double' in one season. There have been great moments for these sides in derbies past and, undoubtedly, will be great moments in years to come. Hopefully, these moments will be on the pitch and not off it and the Swansea teams will come out on the winning side.

Closing thoughts

As a youngster, I never imagined that following Swansea City would let me experience so many emotions. To coin the old phrase, it has been 'one large rollercoaster ride'. I can remember promotion to Division One and subsequent relegation all the way back down. There's been a Wembley win and a Wembley defeat. Play-off heartbreak, famous cup victories, European games, local derbies, good managers and bad managers. Some great players have worn the white shirt and some players I would rather forget.

Emotions like these do not happen to supporters of every club and it's memories like these that should make us proud to be Swansea supporters. Supporting Swansea City is not easy; no one ever promised me that it would be. Think back over the last twenty years and list the number of seasons where we have not been battling relegation, chasing promotion or on a cup run. I promise you, there are not many seasons where we have sat nicely in mid-table with nothing to play for bar pride.

You will have seen in this book the range of emotions that supporters feel while watching our team. You will have read completely different accounts of certain games. That is how it should be and what makes football the number one talked about sport – if we all had the same view, there wouldn't be much to talk about.

As we move on into the twenty-first century, we have a team that are the reigning champions of the Third Division. That achievement is something that we can all be proud of. None of us know what the future will hold for this football club of ours. It could be more championship seasons to come; it could be an immediate relegation. Only time will answer this for us. What I do know is that whatever occurs on the pitch, there will be the creation of more memories and more stories of Swansea City Football Club. Be they good, bad or indifferent they will be there and in themselves they will fill another book.

I hope that you have enjoyed the selection of stories and memories that we have bought together for you in *Voices of Vetch Field*. The selection of the articles was a long and rewarding one and I lost count of the times I lost myself in my own memories whilst reading them. Many people contributed to the compilation of the book and I wish that I had the time to thank each of them individually.

There were many more stories that we have left out – probably enough to fill another book or two. All these stories were valuable in their own right but sadly space didn't permit us to share them with you all. We have a great football club, with a fantastic history that is bettered by few clubs on this earth. All I ask is that wherever you may be, whoever you may be with, you always remain proud to be a Swan.

Phil Sumbler